Tom Wright is Professor of the New Testament and Early Christianity at the University of St Andrews. He is the author of over eighty books, including the For Everyone guides to the New Testament and, most recently, *Finding God in the Psalms*, *The Meal Jesus Gave Us*, *Surprised by Scripture*, *Simply Good News*, *God in Public* and *The Day the Revolution Began* (all published by SPCK).

ADVENT
for
EVERYONE

A JOURNEY
WITH THE APOSTLES

TOM
WRIGHT

First published in Great Britain in 2017

Society for Promoting Christian Knowledge
36 Causton Street
London SW1P 4ST
www.spck.org.uk

Scripture quotations are taken from *The New Testament for Everyone*
by Tom Wright, copyright Nicholas Thomas Wright 2011.

British Library Cataloguing-in-Publication Data
A catalogue record for this book is available from the British Library

ISBN 978–0–281–07838–7
eBook ISBN 978–0–281–07839–4

1 3 5 7 9 10 8 6 4 2

Typeset by Manila Typesetting Company, Makati City
Manufacture managed by Jellyfish
Printed in Great Britain by
Ashford Colour Press Ltd

eBook by Manila Typesetting Company, Makati City

Produced on paper from sustainable forests

CONTENTS

INTRODUCTION

As Christmas has become more exhausting and commercialized, many people find that keeping the preparatory season of Advent helps them to stay focused and recover something of the mystery and excitement that Christmas itself ought to have. Many churches now hold special Advent services. As we approach the darkest time of the year (in the northern hemisphere at least), Advent offers a gleam of light. And hope.

But Advent itself can be puzzling. 'Advent' means 'coming' or 'arrival'. The hymns and readings often used during this season seem to be about two quite different things: about waiting for the 'first coming', the birth of Jesus, and about waiting for his 'second coming' to put everything right in the end. How did these things get muddled up? How can we make wise, prayerful sense out of it all?

The early Christians developed the 'church's year' as a way of telling, learning and reliving the story of Jesus, which stands at the heart of our faith. As they did so, they came to understand that it wasn't simply a matter of going round and round the same sequence and never getting anywhere. Think of a bicycle wheel; it goes round and round, but it is moving forwards, not standing still. The same circuit around the hub of the wheel becomes part of the forward movement of the bicycle as a whole. So it is with the church's year. We go round the circuit: Advent, Christmas, Epiphany, Lent, Holy Week and Good Friday, Easter, Pentecost. The traditional Western churches sum all this up on Trinity Sunday, as we learn more deeply who our glorious God really is. But the point of it all is that, in doing this, we are not simply going round and round the same topics and never getting anywhere. We are signing on as part of God's larger project, God's forward purposes, his plans for the whole creation to be renewed, so that (as the prophets said) the earth will be full of the knowledge and glory of the Lord, as the waters cover the sea. In Jesus, God brought heaven and earth together; in his second coming, that joining together will be complete. That is the Advent hope.

So the church's year overlaps with itself. In Advent, we think our way back to the ancient people of God, to the call of Abraham and his family as the start of God's rescue operation for a world in ruins and a human race in chaos. We follow the story of Israel's hope, a hope that refused to die no matter what terrible things happened; a hope that the first Christians believed had become human in the baby Jesus. With that 'first Advent', it was clear that God's rescue operation for humans and the world had been decisively begun but not yet completed. Jesus really did launch God's kingdom 'on earth as in heaven' in his public career, his death and his resurrection. But it was clear, because of the sort of thing this kingdom was, that it would then need to make its way through the humble, self-giving service of Jesus' followers, until the time when Jesus returned to finish the work, to put all things right, to banish evil and death for ever, and to bring heaven and earth completely together.

The 'second Advent', then, overlaps with the first. We celebrate Jesus' first coming, and use that sense of fulfilment to fuel our hope for his second coming and to strengthen us to work for signs of that kingdom in our own day. We live between the first Advent and the second. That is one way of saying what it means to be a follower of Jesus.

The readings in the present book have been chosen to help you ponder and pray through what all this means: what it meant at the time (we always have to go back to that to check our bearings) and what it means today and tomorrow (we always have to come forward to that to stay on track). My hope and prayer is that this book will help individuals, groups and churches to be 'Advent people': people of light in a dark world, people of hope in times and places of despair. People who follow Jesus.

WEEK 1: A TIME FOR THANKSGIVING

FIRST SUNDAY OF ADVENT

Thankful for God's Grace: 1 Corinthians 1.3–9

[3]Grace to you and peace from God our father and King Jesus the Lord.

[4]I always thank my God for you, for the grace of God that was given to you in King Jesus. [5]You were enriched in him in everything, in every kind of speech and knowledge, [6]just as the messianic message was established among you, [7]so that you aren't missing out on any spiritual gift as you wait eagerly for our Lord, King Jesus, to be revealed. [8]He will establish you right through to the end, so that you are blameless on the day of our Lord, King Jesus. [9]God is faithful! And it is through God that you have been called into the fellowship of his son, King Jesus, our Lord.

We weren't long into the phone call before I noticed something was different. It was the first time I'd spoken to this friend for some weeks and, whichever way the conversation turned, one name kept coming up. She and James had been talking over dinner last night . . . James was hoping to get promotion soon and would be working much closer to where she lived . . . perhaps I knew so-and-so who'd been at school with James? . . . and so on, and so on. There was a warmth, an excitement, and the conclusion was obvious; any minute now, she hoped, James would ask the key question, to which her answer was ready and waiting.

Well, it happened, of course, and they are now married, but my point is to notice how people give themselves away by what they go on talking about, almost (it sometimes appears) to the point of obsession. It doesn't take long in someone's company, or even during a phone call, before you discover what's really exciting them: what is at the centre of their waking thoughts.

If we had any doubts what Paul was excited about, what was at the centre of his thoughts and intentions, this first paragraph of one of his most varied and lengthy letters would soon put us straight. One name keeps coming up, over and over again: Jesus. The name occurs eight times in these nine verses. Paul couldn't stop talking about Jesus, because without Jesus nothing else he said or did made any sense. And what he wanted the Corinthians to get hold of most of all is what it means to have Jesus at the middle of your story, your life, your thoughts, your imagination. If they could do that, all the other issues that rush to and fro through the letter would sort themselves out.

In particular, he wanted them to have Jesus at the centre of their understanding of the world and of history. Most of the Christians in Corinth had not been Jews but ordinary 'pagans'. They had been Gentiles, believing in various gods and goddesses, but without any idea that history, the story of the world, was *going* anywhere or that their own lives might be part of that forward movement. Again and again Paul wants them to learn this lesson: that they have been caught up into a great movement of the love and power of the one true God, the God of Israel, whose work for the whole world has now been unveiled through the events concerning his son. That's why Jesus is at the centre of the picture.

Look how, with a few deft strokes of the pen, he sketches a picture of the Christians in Corinth so that, at every point, their story is intertwined with Jesus' story. To begin with, God has set them aside for his own special purposes in King Jesus; that's what 'called to be holy' in verse 2 means. I don't possess very many suits, but there is one I keep for best, which only comes out on the most special of occasions. That's what being 'holy' means, from God's point of view; it means that he has set people aside for special purposes; and the people in question are expected to cooperate with this.

But once they've been set aside as special, they discover that they are part of a large and growing worldwide family, brothers and sisters of everyone who 'calls on the name of our Lord King Jesus'. In fact, 'calling on' his name is the one and only sign of membership in this family, though people in Paul's day and ever since have tried to introduce other signs of membership as well. And the idea of 'calling on his name' links this worldwide family back to the earlier story of Israel, the people who 'called on the name of the Lord' in the sense of the Lord YHWH, Israel's God. Right from the start, Paul shows what's going on: in Jesus, Israel's true king, the world's true Lord, Israel's one God has become personally present in the world, summoning all people into his family.

As in most of his letters, Paul follows the opening greeting by telling the Corinthians what he thanks God for when he thinks of them. Notice how he moves from what has happened to them in the past, through the sort of people they are in the present and on to the hope they have for the future, with Jesus at the centre at every stage. God has given them his 'grace' in King Jesus (verse 4). 'Grace' is one of those little words that contains a whole universe of meaning, summing up the fact that God loved them and acted decisively on their behalf even though they had done nothing whatever to deserve it, but rather the opposite.

The result of this 'grace' is that God's riches have enriched them (verses 5, 6). They have become a community of learners, growing eagerly in knowledge about God and his new life, able to teach one another, and so strengthening and confirming the original royal proclamation, 'the messianic message', that has been made to them.

God has called them in the past, God equips them in the present and God will complete the process in the future. World history, and the story of the Christian life, has a shape, and Jesus is its shaper at every point. There is coming a day – like 'the day of the Lord' in the Old Testament, only more so – when the hidden truth about the world will be unveiled; this truth will turn out to be a person, and the person will turn out to be Jesus. That's why it's the central Christian badge or sign to 'call on him', to pray to the father through him, to know his friendship and love, and to thank him for the wonderful grace he has given us – yesterday, today and for ever.

For Reflection or Discussion

In what ways do you see your church as part of a worldwide family? How does this enable you to 'call on' Jesus?

WEEK 1: MONDAY

Thanksgiving in Suffering: 2 Corinthians 1.8–11

[8]You see, my dear family, we don't want to keep you in the dark about the suffering we went through in Asia. The load

4

we had to carry was far too heavy for us; it got to the point where we gave up on life itself. ⁹Yes: deep inside ourselves we received the death sentence. This was to stop us relying on ourselves, and to make us rely on the God who raises the dead. ¹⁰He rescued us from such a great and deadly peril, and he'll do it again; we have placed our hope in him, that he'll do it again! ¹¹But you must co-operate with us through prayer for us, so that when God gives us this gift, answering the prayers of so many, all the more will give thanks because of what's happened to us.

You watch from a distance as a friend walks down the street. You see him turn and go into a house. He strides in cheerfully and purposefully. You wait for a few minutes. Then you see him come out again – only now you see, to your horror, that he is limping, staggering along, with bruises on his face and blood trickling from one arm. You are filled with pity and sympathy, but also with puzzlement: *What on earth happened in that house?*

The historian, particularly the ancient historian, is often in the position of the puzzled spectator. We may have evidence about an early phase of someone's career and then again a later phase, but what happened in between is often hidden from us. So it is with Paul. He has gone into the house, striding cheerfully along; that is how he appears to us in 1 Corinthians. Now, in 2 Corinthians, we see him emerge again, battered and bruised. Even his style of writing seems to have changed. But we don't know what happened inside.

Nor does he tell us. Like many people in the ancient world, he was more interested in what illness or suffering *meant* than in giving us a detailed account of his symptoms. Most of what we know is in these verses; we can glean a little from things he says later in the letter, but it doesn't amount to much. He simply refers to 'the suffering we went through in Asia' (the Roman province of 'Asia' was roughly the western half of modern Turkey, with Ephesus in the middle of its west coast; Ephesus was where Paul was staying when he wrote 1 Corinthians). What had happened?

Acts doesn't help at this point, either. Perhaps, if Paul was imprisoned and ill-treated in Ephesus – as seems likely – the author of Acts was anxious not to draw too much attention to it. He has Paul getting into enough trouble as it is. But the riot in the theatre in Ephesus, which Acts describes in chapter 19, may have been part of it. In that passage, things are quietened down by the city officials. But people had woken up to the fact that if the message Paul was announcing was to catch on, their businesses would suffer; so would their civic pride in the great temple of Diana. And the opposition may well have continued in new and nastier ways, leaving Paul feeling, as he says here, that he's received the sentence of death.

In fact, his description sounds much like what we would call a nervous breakdown. The load had become too heavy; all his natural human resources of energy and strength were worn down to nothing. It's bad enough to hear a magistrate declare that you are sentenced to death; it's far worse when a voice deep inside yourself tells you that you might as well give up and die. That is the point Paul had reached, the point where the night had become totally dark and all hope of dawn had disappeared.

Does that mean he'd been relying on his own resources up to that point? That seems strange for someone who

6

could write, in the previous letter, about his work being done not by his own efforts, but by God's grace (1 Corinthians 15.10). But maybe, beneath this conscious sense of God's help and grace, there was still more that Paul had to learn about the meaning of the resurrection – the very thing that he had made the climax of the earlier letter (chapter 15)! Here he says it plainly: the fact that he came to the point where he despaired of life itself was somehow intended – intended by God, he must mean – to make him rely on 'the God who raises the dead'. This old Jewish belief in the life-giving God, the God whose power created the world and will recreate it, came home freshly to Paul as he found himself stripped of all other resources.

Paul begins his letter by telling them this much, not simply in order to gain sympathy, though no doubt that is part of it, but for two other reasons as well, one which he mentions and one he doesn't. The one he mentions is that he wants them to be bound to him all the more tightly in a fellowship of prayer. When two people or communities pray seriously for one another, a bond is set up between them that transforms their relationship when they meet again. In addition, Paul sees in verse 11 that something else happens, which is what he is really interested in: when lots of people are praying for something and God then grants it, the thanksgiving is increased.

For Paul, when human beings give thanks to God, something at the heart of the universe comes back into proper shape. Humans thanking the creator for his goodness are a symptom of the way the world was meant to be, a sign that one day it really will be like that. And such signs are themselves powerful in helping forward the work of the gospel through which the great day will come.

For Reflection or Discussion

Have you ever reached the point when you felt like giving up? How in those circumstances did you find your way back to God?

WEEK 1: TUESDAY

Grace, Generosity and Gratitude: 2 Corinthians 9.6–15

[6]This is what I mean: someone who sows sparingly will reap sparingly as well. Someone who sows generously will reap generously. [7]Everyone should do as they have determined in their heart, not in a gloomy spirit or simply because they have to, since 'God loves a cheerful giver'. [8]And God is well able to lavish all his grace upon you, so that in every matter and in every way you will have enough of everything, and may be lavish in all your own good works, [9]just as the Bible says:

> They spread their favours wide, they gave to the poor,
> Their righteousness endures for ever.

[10]The one who supplies 'seed to be sown and bread to eat' will supply and increase your seed, and multiply the yield of your righteousness. [11]You will be enriched in every way in all single-hearted goodness, which is working through us to produce thanksgiving to God. [12]The service of this ministry will not only supply what God's people so badly need, but it will also overflow with many thanksgivings to God. [13]Through meeting the test of this service you will glorify God in two ways: first, because your confession of faith in

8

the Messiah's gospel has brought you into proper order, and second, because you have entered into genuine and sincere partnership with them and with everyone. [14]What's more, they will then pray for you and long for you because of the surpassing grace God has given to you. [15]Thanks be to God for his gift, the gift we can never fully describe!

Imagine trying to pack an umbrella into a cardboard tube. If you try putting the handle in first it will be difficult. Even if the handle is straight, you will find that the metal tips of the umbrella's struts get caught on the edge of the tube as you struggle to push it in. You may eventually succeed, but you are likely to tear the umbrella, or perhaps the cardboard, in the attempt. The answer, of course, is to turn the umbrella round so that the pointed end goes in first. Then, even if the umbrella isn't folded up properly, you will find that it goes in easily enough.

Something similar happens when people try to persuade others into a course of action that they may find difficult or challenging. Going on telling people to do something they don't particularly want to do is like pushing an umbrella into a tube the wrong way round. You may succeed; if you're a forceful enough character, people may eventually do what you want. But they won't enjoy it and you may damage some relationships on the way. The trick is to turn people's minds and imaginations around so that what seemed forced, awkward and unnatural now seems the most natural thing of all.

Paul rounds off his careful and cautious appeal about the collection by standing back from the details of travel plans and other arrangements and outlining the worldview within which generous giving of the sort he has in mind no longer seems awkward or peculiar. It would be easy to read this passage as simply a list of wise maxims, shrewd and pithy sayings about human generosity and God's abundant goodness; but, although the passage does have that flavour, there is more to it than that. It may be just a sketch, but it's a sketch of nothing less than the whole picture of what it means to be God's people. Give people a few slogans, and you may end up simply trying to force them to do things they don't want to. Turn their minds around so that they see everything – God, the world, the church, themselves – in a different light, and the behaviour may come naturally.

As always, Paul's vision of God's people is firmly rooted in the Bible. And whenever Paul quotes a passage of the Bible, even four or five words, it's worth looking at the original passage, often the entire chapter or paragraph from which the quotation is taken, and seeing what its overall sense is. Here we have three passages, each one of which contributes more than meets the eye to what he is saying, and that together help him to construct a larger picture of who God's people are, what their goal in life should be and how generosity in giving plays a vital part in it all.

The first passage he quotes is from a verse in Proverbs that occurs in the Greek translation of Proverbs 22.9: 'God blesses a cheerful giver.' Paul and his churches would normally have read the Bible in Greek and the passage he quotes would have been part of that Bible, even though (for reasons that are now difficult to fathom) it isn't in the Hebrew texts and, in consequence, isn't in the English and other translations we know today. But what's more important is that much of Proverbs 22 as a whole is about riches and poverty, which has of course been Paul's subject now for two chapters of this letter. 'A good name', Proverbs 22 begins, 'is to be chosen instead of great riches, and grace is better than silver and gold.' Paul has been talking about 'grace' a good deal in these chapters and the 'grace' in question often consists precisely in living for the good name of being God's people rather than hanging on for dear life to silver and gold. Several subsequent verses give instruction about riches. Verse 8 speaks of people who 'sow' wickedness and 'reap' evil, while verse 9 speaks of those who take pity on the poor being themselves supplied with food. Paul is, as often, calling to mind an entire passage, not just a single saying, since he starts his own passage by talking about people 'sowing' in a meagre way or a generous way; and the word he uses for 'generously' is the same word used in Proverbs ('blesses') for what God will do to a cheerful giver. Proverbs gives a reasonably complete portrait of a wise and God-fearing person who knows how to be generous with money. Paul wants the Corinthians to see this as a portrait of themselves.

The second passage he quotes from is Psalm 112.9, speaking again of the person who scatters blessing to the poor. Such a person, says the Psalm, has a 'righteousness' that lasts for ever. This word 'righteousness' is a puzzle to many today, since it makes people think of that unpleasant quality, 'self-righteousness'. But it's hard to know what other word to use. In the Psalms and elsewhere in the Old Testament, it regularly refers on the one hand to God's own faithfulness to the promises he made to his people, and on the other to the behaviour by which God's people demonstrate their gratitude to God for this faithfulness. In the case of the present Psalm, the whole poem is a celebration of those who fear and trust the Lord, and in particular of their generosity and merciful behaviour towards their neighbours, especially the poor. Once again, Paul is inviting the Corinthians to step inside the biblical portrait and discover a whole new identity, not simply to do something strange because he tells them to.

But the real climax comes in the third passage. God, says Paul, provides 'seed for the sower and bread to eat', quoting Isaiah 55.10. Isaiah 55 is the glorious invitation to all and sundry to come and feast on God's rich bounty, because God is making a new creation in which everything will be renewed. This new creation, achieved through the death and resurrection of the Servant of the Lord in Isaiah 53, is based on the covenant renewal celebrated in Isaiah 54 and will come about because God will 'sow' his Word in the same way that he sends rain and snow to provide seed-corn and bread.

What Paul is urging the Corinthians to do is think of themselves, as it were, this way round and discover that, if they realize they are characters in the great drama which is going forward, then the generosity he is urging will come naturally. In the normal and healthy Christian life, everything proceeds from God's generosity, and everything returns to God in thanksgiving. Grace, generosity and gratitude: these are not optional extras of Christian living, but are the very heart of it all.

For Reflection or Discussion

Are you a cheerful giver? How do you think Paul's words might help you give more generously?

WEEK 1: WEDNESDAY

Prayer for Wisdom and Gratitude: Colossians 1.9–14

⁹For this reason, from the day we heard it, we haven't stopped praying for you. We're asking God to fill you with the knowledge of what he wants in all wisdom and spiritual understanding. ¹⁰This will mean that you'll be able to conduct yourselves in a manner worthy of the Lord, and so give him real delight, as you bear fruit in every good work and grow up in the knowledge of God. ¹¹I pray that you'll be given all possible strength, according to the power of his glory, so that you'll have complete patience and become truly steadfast and joyful.

¹²And I pray that you will learn to give thanks to the father, who has made you fit to share the inheritance of God's holy ones in the light. ¹³He has delivered us from the power of darkness, and transferred us into the kingdom of his beloved son. ¹⁴He is the one in whom we have redemption, the forgiveness of sins.

We watched, holding our breath, as the mother duck left the pond at the head of her brood. There were seven ducklings in all: four black ones and three yellow ones. They were lively and squeaky, scuttling to and fro. For days they had swum about with their mother in the little pond. Now it was time for her to take them to the nearby lake.

This meant danger. To get there they had to cross a main road and make their way through a park where dogs, cats, larger birds and several other predators would be watching. Fortunately, in this city at least, local residents are prepared for this moment and make sure that traffic comes to a stop to let the little procession pass through. They reached their destination safely. But we were left marvelling at the mother's apparent calm confidence as she led her little family through potential hazards and on to the larger world where she would then bring them up to maturity.

Paul, in prison in Ephesus, must often have felt like a mother duck. Here was he in a little church, just starting up, full of energy and enthusiasm but hardly yet aware of the great dangers and problems that were to be faced. He couldn't even be with them in person to guide them and teach them. The mother duck has to rely on instinct – her own, and that of her recently born babies – to see them through. But ordinary human instinct alone won't get the young church through to maturity. Human instincts are important, but they remain earthbound. When people become Christians, God implants into them a new sense of his presence and love, his guiding and strengthening. This sense needs nurturing and developing. New Christians need to understand what's happening to them, and how they must cooperate with the divine life that's gently begun to work in them.

Paul, in prison, can help this process in two ways: by writing, as he is doing, but supremely by prayer. He may not be with the Colossians in person. But the God who is with them is also with him, and in the mystery (and hard work) of prayer he can help their progress towards Christian maturity.

The foundation of what he prays for is that the new Christian instinct may become firmly implanted in them. Just as the mother duck wants her brood to be able to work out for themselves how to feed, to avoid danger and to live wisely in a threatening environment, so Paul longs to see young Christians coming to know for themselves what God's will is (verse 9). They need 'wisdom and spiritual understanding'; not just book-learning (though some of that may help) or human traditions (though they are often useful, too), but a deep inner sense of who they now are, of the newly created human life which they have received from God, and of what will nurture it or harm it. Christian teachers can talk till they're blue in the face, but unless their hearers have this inner sense of wisdom and understanding, this awareness of the true God loving them and shaping their lives in a new way, it won't produce genuine disciples.

With that in place, however, Paul's prayer passes to two other things: behaviour and bearing fruit (verse 10). The new instinct implanted in the Christian will lead him or her to a new lifestyle, which delights God not least because it reflects at last his glorious intention for his human creatures.

But if this is to happen, the new life that's been implanted in Christians has to show itself in the form of energy, power and strength to live in the new way. That, too, is promised, and that too is what Paul is praying for. God's power has already delivered us from the kingdom of darkness and transferred us into the kingdom of his son, Jesus. That same power is now available to continue the work of bringing our lives into conformity with the new world which opens up before us.

When Paul speaks of God rescuing people from one kingdom and giving them another one, and of 'redemption' and 'forgiveness' as the central themes of that rescue operation, he has the exodus from Egypt in mind. What God has done in Jesus, and is now doing for them, is the new exodus, the great moment of setting the slaves free.

To become a Christian is to leave the 'Egypt' of sin and to travel gratefully towards the promised inheritance.

Why 'gratefully'? Because the climax of Paul's prayer is that the young Christians will learn the art of thanksgiving. What Paul most wants to see growing in the church, as a sign of healthy Christian life on the way to maturity, is gratitude to God for the extraordinary things he's done in Jesus, and the remarkable things he is continuing to do in the world and in their lives.

Spontaneous gratitude of this kind is a sign that they are coming to know and love the true God, as opposed to some imaginary one. Gods that people invent can't compare with the true one when it comes to overflowing generosity. Paul would say to us, as he said to the young Christians in Colossae, that a life lived in the presence of this God will be a life full of thanksgiving. Or have we forgotten who our God really is?

For Reflection or Discussion

Have you been able to see new Christians in your church growing in God's wisdom? How do you express your gratitude for this?

WEEK 1: THURSDAY

Thanksgiving is Key! 1 Timothy 4.1–5

¹Now the spirit specifically declares that in the last times some people will abandon the faith, and will cling on to deceitful spirits and demonic teachings ²perpetrated by hypocritical false teachers whose consciences are branded with a hot iron. ³They will forbid marriage, and teach people to abstain from

foods which God created to be received with thanksgiving by people who believe and know the truth. [4]Every creation of God, you see, is good; nothing is to be rejected if it is received with thanksgiving, [5]for then it is made holy by God's word and prayer.

Jane grew up in a family which was always playing games. Outdoor games, whenever possible; but if the weather was bad, and especially on long winter evenings, the children would curl up around the fire and play – well, you name it: Scrabble, Monopoly, Cluedo, of course, and lots of other board games. But best of all they liked the old-fashioned card games. They liked the feel of the cards; the excitement of having them dealt out and look-ing eagerly to see whether they'd got a good hand or not. They got to know the different faces of the jack, queen and king of each suit, and the most special cards of all, the aces. They even had nicknames for them. In later years they would look back and realize that what they might have missed out on, in those days before televi-sion, they had more than made up for in terms of exer-cising their memories, their ability to think strategically and, equally important, their readiness to play the hand they'd been dealt and not grumble because someone else had a better one.

It was only when Jane met James and got to know his family that she realized for the first time that not every-body saw playing cards in that way. James's grandfather had lost his job in the Depression, and the family had had to move into a small house in a shabby neighbourhood. In desperation, casting about wildly for some way to recover financial stability and provide for his family, he had gone onc cvcning into a bar where people were gambling for money. But what began as a last desperate measure quickly became an obsession. The jack, queen and king imprisoned him in their castle, and he broke the hearts of his family instead of bringing them back the diamonds he had hoped. James's father had grown up in a household where the very sight of playing cards reminded them of folly, shame, ridicule and ruin.

Now of course people can, and do, gamble on anything. And some people, it seems, can have (as they say) a mild 'flutter' on horses, dogs, cards or whatever without it becoming a habit, let alone a destructive one. But social fashions have associated some things so closely with gambling, and gambling so closely with irresponsible, immoral and ruinous behaviour, that the very objects themselves – pasteboard cards with lifeless decorations – have been seen by some as 'tainted' and so to be avoided.

This helps us to understand the position Paul is describing in verses 2 and 3, and the teaching he offers against it in verses 4 and 5. In the early church, and in many later periods of Christianity, there were some people whose experience of the pagan world had been very destructive. In particular, they had been used to engaging in wild and profligate sex, drunken orgies of various kinds. Modern as well as ancient experience suggests that when people go in for that kind of behaviour in a serious way it turns out to be destructive, and they know in their bones that this is not how humans were made to live. Something in you dies when you give yourself indiscriminately to gluttony, whether in food, drink or sex. And we can easily understand – not least because several people have written frankly about it in their own experience – that people who go that route may well end up hating the very thought of good food, of alcoholic drinks, or indeed of sex. People like that, Paul says, have had their consciences branded as though with a hot iron. The inner guiding light that ought to be telling them that some things are good and other things are bad has been so mistreated that it now winces with pain at the very thought of some things which are perfectly all right in themselves, part of the good creation of a good creator God.

This, in fact, is the underlying point, and it needs making again and again in almost every generation. If in doubt, read Genesis 1: God saw all that he made, *and it was very good.* That is the foundation of all genuine Christian (and for that matter Jewish) thinking. Anything which implies that some part of the created order is bad in itself is the first swish of the axe which will cut off the branch on which we should be sitting – the belief that the God who made the world in the first place is remaking it through Jesus and the spirit, and that we are called, not to abandon our humanity but to celebrate its rescue, redemption and remaking. What we see in this passage is one of the early signs of a problem which dogged the footsteps of Christian thinkers through much of the early period, and reappears from time to time today.

In particular, it's fascinating that already by the time of this letter Paul could see that some would end up saying that sex itself is simply bad, so that ideally all people should be celibate. Some have even charged Paul himself with taking this view, though a more careful reading of 1 Corinthians 7, the key passage, will show how wrong that is. And when it came to food and drink,

Paul took the robust view that *nothing* was unclean in itself – including the foods that the Old Testament had prohibited, and including meat that had been offered in sacrifice to idols. That's the point of 1 Corinthians 8—10, though as that passage makes clear he is equally insistent that Christians must give up their rights to eat whatever they like if it weakens the faith of another Christian. But the underlying point is the one to grasp: creation is good; created pleasures, in their proper and appropriate form and context, are to be received with thanksgiving.

Thanksgiving is more than just a recognition of the fact that we receive everything from the hands of a loving God. It is the fundamental human and Christian stance, poised between God and creation. It simultaneously renounces idolatry – treating the created order as if it were itself divine – and the dualism which treats creation as shabby or bad. When we thank God, we grow to our proper stature. That's why those who reject creation, just like those who idolize it, must be seen as deceitful and even demonic (verse 1). Finding our way down the straight path between worshipping creation and rejecting it may be difficult from time to time. But thanksgiving – coupling God's word, which affirms the goodness of creation, with grateful prayer – is the key to it all.

For Reflection or Discussion

Is there any part of creation you reject through having overindulged? How does Paul suggest you might reclaim pleasure in it?

WEEK 1: FRIDAY

A Call for Gratitude: Hebrews 12.25–29

[25]Take care that you don't refuse the one who is speaking. For if people didn't escape when they rejected the one who gave them earthly warnings, how much more if we turn away from the one who speaks from heaven! [26]At that point, his voice shook the earth; but now he has issued a promise in the following words: 'One more time I will shake not only the earth but heaven as well.' [27]The phrase 'one more time' shows that the things that are to be shaken (that is, the created things) will be taken away, so that the things that cannot be shaken will remain.

[28]Well, then: we are to receive a kingdom which cannot be shaken! This calls for gratitude! That's how to offer God true and acceptable worship, reverently and with fear. [29]Our God, you see, is a devouring fire.

The first time I stayed in a hotel in Los Angeles, I was startled by the polite little card on the table beside the television. I am quite used to fire regulations, instructions about laundry and advertisements for room service, but this was different. It was headed 'What to Do in Case of an Earthquake'. All I now remember of it is that I was supposed to hide under the table in case the ceiling fell in. Much good that would be, I thought, since I was on the twenty-third floor. But fortunately the night passed without any tremors or wobbles, and the really interesting question – whether there was enough space under the table for someone of my size to fit – went unanswered.

A real earthquake is of course, along with fire and flood, one of the most frightening events anyone can experience. For so much of normal life we take for granted the stability of the earth, the roads and the walls and roofs of the houses we live in. An earthquake faces people not only with sudden and severe physical danger but also with the deeper shock of realizing that, quite literally, the foundations of their world are not as secure as they thought they were. The Lisbon earthquake of 1755 offered a challenge of yet a further dimension, in that people had been accustomed to speak of the created world as being basically a stable, good place where God looked after people's well-being. Suddenly all that was thrown into question, precipitating a flood of books, poems and philosophical musings on what became known as 'natural evil'.

The really worrying thing in the present passage, though, is that the promise of the earth, and heaven too, being shaken comes directly from God, as part of his plan to take his creation by the scruff of the neck and make it, at last, what he always intended it would be. As Revelation 21 insists, for there to be new heavens and a new earth the present heavens, as well as the present earth, must undergo their own radical change, almost like a death and new birth.

Hebrews uses a different image for this transition, but the end result is the same. Heaven and earth alike must be 'shaken' in such a way that everything transient, temporary, secondary and second-rate may fall away. Then that which is of the new creation, based on Jesus himself and his resurrection, will shine out the more brightly. This new creation will, of course, include all those who belong to the new covenant, and, through them, the new world which God has always promised.

This breathtaking assurance of God's new world comes to the readers not only as promise, though, but also as warning. If people who refused to listen to Moses found themselves in dire trouble, what will happen if people now refuse to listen to one who is so much greater than Moses?

You will not find in Hebrews any sentimental pictures of God as an indulgent parent, always there to comfort, never wanting to make too much of a fuss. The true God is not tame, nor does he spoil his children. He is like a fire: the holiness of God, emphasized through the Temple ritual, is not undermined by the fact that, in the new covenant, his people are invited into his presence in a new way. To think like that would be to make a radical mistake. It isn't that God has stopped being holy. God hasn't changed a bit. It is, rather, that Jesus has opened a new and living path, through the 'curtain' and right up to him. Only when we remind ourselves of God's holiness do we fully appreciate the significance of what Jesus achieved.

The appropriate response to all this is gratitude and worship. True gratitude, both for the present world and for the world to come, is the deepest and truest form of worship, reaching places which the entire sacrificial system never could. When you bow down before the living God and thank him from the bottom of your heart for what he's done and for what he will do, it is as though you are a priest in the Temple, offering the purest, most unblemished sacrifice. Only much, much more so. That is the privilege of being a follower of Jesus the Messiah. That is the life to which our fiery God now calls us.

For Reflection or Discussion

Have you ever found your world shaken to its foundations by God? What ways have you found to express gratitude for this?

WEEK 1: SATURDAY

Praise and Thanks to the Creator: Revelation 4.6b–11

[6b]In the middle of the throne, and all around the throne, were four living creatures, full of eyes in front and behind. [7]The first creature was like a lion, the second creature was like an ox, the third creature had a human face, and the fourth creature was like a flying eagle. [8]Each of the four creatures had six wings, and they were full of eyes all round and inside. Day and night they take no rest, as they say,

'Holy, holy, holy,
Lord God Almighty,
Who Was and Who Is and Who Is to Come.'

[9]When the creatures give glory and honour and thanksgiving to the one who is sitting on the throne, the one who lives for ever and ever, [10]the twenty-four elders fall down in front of the one who is sitting on the throne, and worship the one who lives for ever and ever. They throw down their crowns in front of the throne, saying, [11]'O Lord our God, you deserve to receive glory and honour and power, because you created all things; because of your will they existed and were created.'

Scientists and anthropologists have often asked themselves, 'What is it that humans can do that computers can't do?' Computers, after all, can play chess better than most of us. They can work out answers to all kinds of questions that would take us a lot longer. Some people have boldly declared that, though at the moment computers can't do quite everything that we can, they will one day overtake us.

The writer David Lodge wrote a powerful novel on this theme, entitled *Thinks* . . . The heroine eventually discovers the answer: humans can weep; and humans can forgive. Those are two very powerful and central human activities. They take place in a quite different dimension from anything a computer can do. But without them, we would be less than human.

A similar question is often posed: 'What can humans do that animals can't do?' Again, some scientists have tried to insist that we humans are simply 'naked apes', a more sophisticated version of apes perhaps, but still within the same continuum. This is a trickier question than the one about computers, but to get straight to the point: in our present passage, the main difference is that humans can say the word 'because'. In particular, they can say it about God himself.

Consider the two songs of praise in this passage, the first in verse 8 and the second in verse 11. The first one is the song which the four living creatures sing round the clock, day and night. They praise God as the holy one; they praise him as the everlasting one. The four creatures deserve our attention for other reasons, too. They seem in some ways to resemble the seraphim who surround God in Isaiah's vision in the Temple (Isaiah 6), and they are also quite like the four creatures of Ezekiel's vision (Ezekiel 1). They represent the animal creation, including humans but at this stage with the human-faced creature being simply one among the others, alongside the king of the wild beasts (the lion), the massive leader of tamed animals (the ox) and the undisputed king of the birds (the eagle). (In some early Christian traditions, these animals represent the four gospel writers, so that Matthew (the human face), Mark (the lion), Luke (the ox) and John (the eagle) are thought of as the living creatures who surround, and worship, the Jesus of whom they speak.) These remarkable creatures seem to be not merely surrounding God's throne but ready to do his bidding. Twice John tells us that they are 'full of eyes': unsleeping, keeping watch for God over his whole creation.

The song of these living creatures is simply an act of adoring praise and thanks. We are meant, reading this passage, to see with the Psalmist that all creation is dependent on God and worships him in its own way. That alone is worth pondering as a striking contrast to how most of us view the animal kingdom. But the contrast with the 24 elders is then made all the more striking. Creation as a whole simply worships God; the humans who represent God's people *understand why they do so*. 'You *deserve*', they say, 'to receive glory and honour and power, *because* you created all things.' There it is: the 'because' that distinguishes humans from other animals, however noble those animals may be in their own way. Humans are given the capacity to reflect, to understand what's going on. And, in particular, to express that understanding in worship.

Worship, after all, is the most central human activity. Certainly it's the most central Christian activity. When I was a student, many of us busied ourselves with all kinds of Christian activities – teaching and learning, studying scripture, evangelism, prayer meetings and so on. We went to church quite a lot, but never (I think) reflected much on what we were doing there. There was, after all, a sermon to learn from, and the hymns were good teaching aids as well. It was a time of learning and fellowship. When a friend suggested at one point that worship was actually the centre of everything, the rest of us looked at him oddly. It seemed a bit of a cop-out.

Now, of course, I know he was right. Worship is what we were made for; worship with a *because* in it is what marks us out as genuine human beings.

For Reflection or Discussion

Are you conscious of your vocation to worship with a 'because'? How do you allow your thinking about God to inform your praise?

WEEK 2: A TIME FOR PATIENCE

SECOND SUNDAY OF ADVENT

God's Patience: 2 Peter 3.8–15a

[8]So, beloved, don't forget this one thing, that a single day with the Lord is like a thousand years, and a thousand years like a single day. [9]The Lord is not delaying his promise, in the way that some reckon delay, but he is very patient towards you. He does not want anyone to be destroyed. Rather, he wants everyone to arrive at repentance.

[10]But the Lord's day will come like a thief. On that day the heavens will pass away with a great rushing sound, the elements will be dissolved in fire, and the earth and all the works on it will be disclosed.

[11]Since everything is going to dissolve in this way, what sort of people should you be? You should live lives that are holy and godly, [12]as you look for God's day to appear, and indeed hurry it on its way – the day because of which the heavens will be set on fire and dissolved, and the elements will melt with heat. [13]But we are waiting for new heavens and a new earth, in which justice will be at home. That is what he has promised.

[14]So, my dear family, as you wait for these things, be eager to be found without spot or blemish before him, in peace. [15]And when our Lord waits patiently to act, see that for what it is – salvation!

This week we will think about the patience to which we are called: patience in our dealings with one another; patience with God as we wait for the day of the Lord. But first we must consider God's own patience.

This is, after all, the right way round. We might present a somewhat comical sight, stamping our little feet with impatience while the creator and ruler of the universe calmly goes about his own business, knowing infinitely more than we do about how to run his world. No: the proper perspective is to regard anything that looks to us like 'delay' as an indication not that we have to be patient with God, but that God is having to be patient with us.

Which is just as well. If God were to foreclose on the world, and on ourselves, straight away, what would happen? This was already a theme which Jews before the time of Jesus were pondering, as they agonized over the apparently endless wait for God's promises to be fulfilled. God, they concluded, was holding back the great day, leaving a space for more people to repent, for lives to be transformed, for the world to come to its senses. One should be grateful for this 'patience', not angry with God for failing to hurry up when we wanted him to.

This is very much what Paul has in mind in a passage like Romans 2.1–11. It might be worth looking that up and pondering it; perhaps this is the sort of passage Peter has in mind. For Paul, 'God's kindness is meant to bring you to repentance' (Romans 2.4). But if you don't avail yourself of that opportunity, the result will be the opposite: what you do instead with that time, with that interval before final judgment, will just make matters worse when the day finally arrives (Romans 2.5–11).

This seems to be what Peter is saying, too. 'When our Lord waits patiently to act, see that for what it is – salvation!' (verse 15). God's patience is our opportunity. It is our chance to work on the holy, godly lives we ought to be living. It is our chance, too, to spread the gospel in the world. Since we know that the day is coming, the day when new heavens and new earth will emerge, filled to the brim with God's wonderful justice, his glorious setting-right of all things, we should be working towards that already, here and now.

This is the point where a wrong view of what God intends to do will really damage both our understanding and our behaviour. If we imagine that God wants simply to burn up the present world entirely, leaving us as dis-embodied souls in some kind of timeless 'eternity', then why should we worry about what we do here and now? What does it matter? Why not just enjoy life as best we can and wait for whatever is coming next – which is of course the answer that many philosophies have given, in the first century as well as today. But if God intends to *renew* the heavens and the earth – as Isaiah promised all those years before (Isaiah 65.17; 66.22), then what we do in the present time matters. It matters for us that we are 'without spot or blemish' (verse 14). It matters for God's world as a whole.

For Reflection or Discussion

Do you find it hard to exercise patience? In what ways might you ease your impatience by working towards the day when God will renew heavens and earth?

WEEK 2: MONDAY

Judgment is Coming – So Keep Going! 2 Timothy 4.1–5

[1]This is my solemn charge to you, in the presence of God and King Jesus, who will judge the living and the dead, and by his appearance and his kingdom: [2]announce the word; keep going whether the time is right or wrong; rebuke,

warn and encourage with all patience and explanation. [3]The time is coming, you see, when people won't tolerate healthy teaching. Their ears will start to itch, and they will collect for themselves teachers who will tell them what they want to hear. [4]They will turn away from listening to the truth and will go after myths instead. [5]But as for you, keep your balance in everything! Put up with suffering; do the work of an evangelist; complete the particular task assigned to you.

I was invigilating an exam on a hot summer day. The undergraduates were tired; it was the fourth or fifth exam they had sat already that week, and there were more to come. The sun beat down outside where their friends were waiting to meet them once they had finished. The large clock on the wall moved slowly towards the finishing time.

'You have ten more minutes.' I watched the faces in the room as my voice broke the silence. As usual, there were two quite different responses. Some of the candidates sighed, smiled and sat back. Time was nearly up; not much point trying to do more. Others raised their eyebrows, took a deep breath, and began to write even faster than they had been doing already. Only ten minutes to go! Better get the essay finished. No time to lose.

Examination technique is an odd thing. Some of those who sat back may have known what they were doing. Some of those who wrote even faster may have been disorganized and were simply trying to splash down anything that came into their heads in the vain hope that the examiners might like at least some of it. But I suspected, as I looked around the room, that the first group were simply shrugging their shoulders and giving up, while the second were the ones making the best use of the time.

Paul lived his life with the clock ticking in the background, and he wants Timothy to do the same. Jesus is already enthroned as king of the world, and one day we shall see his royal appearing, the time when the whole world will be held to account. We don't know – we never know – how close to the final day we have come. But we are summoned to live each day, each year, as people ready to give account, ready to face scrutiny, assessment and judgment. For some this might have meant, 'Oh well, it's going to happen soon, so we may as well stop working and give up.' Paul dealt with that attitude in the letters to the Thessalonians. Here he urges Timothy that because judgment is coming it's important to get on with your work.

His description of Timothy's task fits closely with the first part of this passage, where he's talking about the tasks for which the Bible is useful. Timothy must 'announce the word'; as usual, 'the word' here doesn't just mean 'the Bible', though it will include it. 'The word' regularly refers to the Christian message, the announcement of Jesus as Lord, which is itself rooted in the scriptures of Israel – the only 'Bible' the earliest Christians had – and focused on telling what happened to Jesus, ramming home the point that, through his resurrection, he is now installed as king and Lord.

What's more, Timothy must keep going with this task whether the moment seems propitious or not. As a teacher and preacher, I know that some days just don't seem right. You can't always put your finger on it; but sometimes preaching even a simple sermon, giving a straightforward talk, or counselling someone, becomes really difficult. You have to force the words out. There seems to be no energy anywhere; or, worse, a negative energy working against you. At other times it's different: the words flow effortlessly; things come together; you sense an ease and fluency. There are many different reasons why things should sometimes be difficult: political pressure from outside or inside the community, the wrong or right spiritual atmosphere (to what extent has the church been praying for you in your preparation?), unresolved conflict or evil within the congregation. But how easy it is for preachers then to back off, to give up trying to lead their people into further truth and insight, to trim down the ministry of the word to a few scattered reflections . . . often with the shoulder-shrugging comment that nobody likes sermons these days anyway. And how easy, too, for a preacher who knows that what he or she has to say will be unpopular with some members of the church, or will get them into trouble if the local magistrates hear about it, to trim the content of the teaching down to more general platitudes. Paul, of course, will have none of it. Keep going whether the time is right or wrong!

We know from several things Paul says, both here and in 1 Corinthians, that Timothy was young and perhaps inclined to be shy or anxious. He undoubtedly needed this advice. We probably all know people who inflict their own personality and opinions on everyone they meet, in a brash or even bullying way. Some Christians, alas, are like that, and sometimes they justify their behaviour by quoting texts like this. Each of us has to decide which category we fit into and hence which commands are appropriate for us. Perhaps the best rule of thumb is that, if you feel a pressure to tone down or trim down your message, you probably need this advice, whereas if you find yourself eager to get out there and hit people over the head with the Bible, it *may* be that God is calling you to do just that – but it may be that you are using your faith as an excuse to indulge your aggressive personality.

The end of verse 2 is very significant. The teacher or preacher is not just to lay down the law. He or she is to make things clear 'with all patience and explanation'. The word for 'explanation' is the general word for 'teaching', but the point in this passage is that it won't do simply to rebuke people, to warn them about the dangers of their present beliefs or behaviour, or to encourage them to continue on a particular course. You need to explain why this is important, to back up what you say with clear teaching, going down to the roots of the subject. This takes patience – something the aggressive or bullying teacher probably hasn't got.

Paul himself now has a warning for Timothy, a warning which explains why he has to go on with his patient teaching. Quite soon, people within the Christian community won't want the kind of teaching which will make and keep them healthy and strong. Like people being instructed by their doctors to follow a particular diet, they will discover that half of their favourite foods aren't on it, and so will look for different doctors who will advise them to eat and drink what they like.

Timothy must be aware of this danger, and must hold his course firmly. Verse 5 is a sober, realistic statement of what Christian ministry is about. You have received a particular calling; get on with it. Keep your balance. It may be difficult or painful at times, but you didn't sign on in order to have an easy life. Go on announcing Jesus as Lord.

What is required is not success, as the world regards success, but loyalty, perseverance and patience.

For Reflection or Discussion

Do you think you are either too shy or too aggressive when preaching 'the word'? How might Paul's words in this passage help you find a balance between the two?

WEEK 2: TUESDAY

Keep Up the Good Work: Hebrews 6.9–12

[9]Even though we speak in this way, my dear people, we are confident that there are better things to be said about you, things that point to salvation. [10]God is not unjust, after all – and he'd have to be if he forgot your work, and the love you showed for his name, and all the service you have rendered and are still rendering to his holy people. [11]I want to encourage each one of you to show the same energetic enthusiasm for the task of bringing your hope to its full, assured goal. [12]You mustn't become lazy. There are people who are inheriting the promises through faith and patience, and you should copy them!

Sir Francis Drake was one of many Englishmen who became famous during the reign of Elizabeth I. He sailed round the world, crossed the Atlantic many times, was involved in numerous sea battles in various parts of the world, was twice a member of parliament, and, perhaps most famously, defeated the Spanish Armada when it came to attack England in 1588. There are many well-known stories about him: how he insisted on finishing his game of bowls even though the Armada was in sight; how he spread his cloak over a muddy puddle so that the Queen could walk over it without getting her feet wet; how he once tried to claim California as a British possession.

Not so well known, perhaps, but significant in revealing one of the secrets of his life, filled as it was with remarkable achievements, is a prayer he wrote which is still in frequent use in churches today. It sums up more or less exactly the message of this passage from the middle of Hebrews 6:

> O Lord God, when thou givest to thy servants to endeavour any great matter, grant us also to know that it is not the beginning, but the continuing of the same, until it be thoroughly finished, which yieldeth the true glory; through him who for the finishing of thy work laid down his life for us, our Redeemer, Jesus Christ. Amen.

What Drake said there about great works which had to be attempted – he might have been thinking of another long and dangerous sea voyage, or the numerous tasks he undertook to improve the lot of people living in southwest England – Hebrews says about the entire enterprise of living as a Christian. What matters is not so much the beginning, important though that obviously is, but continuing, carrying on until the thing is thoroughly finished. Most of us will recognize the picture and its challenge. Most of us have started projects and got bogged down: learning a new language, trying to lose weight, painting a picture, reading a long and difficult book. Or even, we might add, starting a business, opening a shop or building a house. Often we discover, some way into such projects, that we really aren't cut out for the task we've begun, and then it may be better to put it aside rather than carry on and make things worse. But often, not least when something is really worthwhile, there are several distinct phases to the process: the initial burst of enthusiasm and the excitement of something quite new, the gradual seeping away of energy as we reach the hard grind of carrying on, and then the days, and perhaps the weeks and even years, when we get out of bed without enthusiasm, without desire to work on the project, wishing we could have some other novelty to excite us, but realizing that there is a goal ahead which will make it all worthwhile if only we can put one foot in front of another until we get there.

Living as a Christian is often like that, and the writer of Hebrews knows that his readers may be in just that situation. They have begun well, and by this stage they have already established an impressive track record of service to God and to one another. The picture of Christian life in verse 10 is attractive: a community devoted to hard work in order to put into practice the love which is at the centre of genuine Christian faith, serving one another and all God's people in every way possible. This sort of thing is solid evidence that their beginning was real, that they certainly do belong to God's people; and, according to verses 9 and 10, that God has already taken note of what they've been doing and won't let them fall away at this point. But at the same time – and here is the mystery at the heart of Christian perseverance – just because God will not forget what they've already done, they themselves must make every effort, must avoid all temptations to be lazy, must continue with the life of faith and patience 'until it be thoroughly finished'. They should take note of other people who are doing so (verse 12), and do their best to copy them.

This strange balance between God's faithfulness and human effort needs a word or two of further explanation. Ever since the Reformation in the sixteenth century, many Christians have been taught, quite rightly, that nothing we do can of itself earn God's favour. Grace remains grace; God loves us because he loves us, not because we manage to do a few things to impress him, or to notch up a few points on some heavenly scorecard. But at the same time the whole New Testament, from the teaching of Jesus in the gospels, through the message of Paul in his letters, and on to letters like Hebrews and James and the great book of Revelation, insists that what Christians *do*, having already been grasped by God's free love and grace, and relying in prayer and faith on further grace every step of the way, matters a great deal. Living as a Christian is never a matter of settling back and 'letting God do it all'.

Yes, there are undoubtedly times when, like the children of Israel standing beside the Red Sea, we need the message that says, 'The Lord will fight for you; all you need to do is to be still' (Exodus 14.14). But these are the exceptional moments, the particular situations, often in times of emergency, when there is nothing we can or should do, and we must trust that God will do it all. But the normal Christian life is one of energy, enthusiasm, faithful effort and patient hard work. It is tragic when people are deceived, by an insistence that God must do it all, into a lazy attitude which shrugs its shoulders and refuses to lift a finger.

Of course – and here Paul and Hebrews are equally insistent – when people patiently work hard both at serving one another and at their own holiness of life, they will usually be aware, and if they aren't they must remind themselves, of where the energy comes from. When Paul tells the Philippians to 'work out their own salvation with fear and trembling', he at once explains by adding that 'God himself is the one that's at work among you' (Philippians 2.12–13). The energy to do all that we are called to do comes itself from God working within us in the power of the holy spirit. The spirit applies to our lives the promises of God in the past (as the writer immediately goes on to say in Hebrews 6.13–20) and the completed work of Jesus the Messiah. This work goes down into our thoughts, our imaginations and (not least) our wills. That's the mystery – the same mystery, of divine and human action, which we meet at so many points of Christian thinking and living.

The important thing, then, is not to wait until you *feel like* living a holy life, or loving your neighbour, or working at the project of Christian service to which you are called and on which you've made a start. Your feelings are as unreliable as tomorrow morning's weather. (I write as an Englishman used to changeable weather all year round, not as, say, a southern Californian knowing that tomorrow, like today, will be sunny and warm!) What matters is the call of the gospel, the promise of God, and your task of being faithful and patient in the present, 'until it be thoroughly finished'.

For Reflection or Discussion

Are there any points in your Christian life when you feel you have taken on a task you are unable to complete? How did you get through it, and how might Paul's words have helped you?

WEEK 2: WEDNESDAY

Looking to Jesus: Hebrews 12.1–3

[1]What about us, then? We have such a great cloud of witnesses all around us! What we must do is this: we must put aside each heavy weight, and the sin which gets in the way so easily. We must run the race that lies in front of us, and we must run it patiently. [2]We must look ahead, to Jesus. He is the one who carved out the path for faith, and he's the one who brought it to completion.

He knew that there was joy spread out and waiting for him. That's why he endured the cross, making light of its shame, and has now taken his seat at the right hand of God's throne. [3]He put up with enormous opposition from sinners. Weigh up in your minds just how severe it was; then you won't find yourselves getting weary and worn out.

I went to a school that prided itself on its outdoor pursuits. Set high in the Yorkshire Dales in north-west England, it celebrated its location in several ways, the annual climax being a ten-mile cross-country race over steep, difficult ground. Often as many as eighty or a hundred boys would enter this race, with the purpose for most of us being not to win – we left that to the serious athletes – but to get round in a reasonable time, to forge on through mud and heather until we made it back to the finish in the small town where the school was situated. The year I ran in the race I came, if I remember rightly, about thirty-fifth; respectable though undistinguished. But the thing I remember most vividly was the final stretch, the last half mile or so. I had trained for the race over the previous weeks, and had been round the actual course several times. I was quite used to the closing stages: here we were, back again, almost at the point of a rest and a bath and a hot drink. But this time it was totally different. I had known there would be spectators, of course, but I hadn't prepared myself for the hundreds of boys, parents and local people from the town who turned out to watch as we all came back, bedraggled but mostly happy, from an hour and a half of hard work. They were cheering, waving flags, clapping and shouting encouragement and congratulations. It went on and on, down the road into the town, increasing as we got to the middle, reaching an extraordinary roar as, with a friend running beside me, I rounded the final bend and came down the road to the finish. All these people! Where had they all come from? And such noise! It felt like being a real celebrity, if only for two minutes.

Several aspects of this climactic passage in Hebrews draw on the image of the Christian pilgrimage as a long-distance race, and the first is, obviously, the 'great cloud of witnesses' all around us. Those who have gone before us, from Abel and Abraham right through to the unnamed heroes and heroines noted at the end of chapter 11, haven't simply disappeared. They are there at the finishing line, cheering us on, surrounding us with encouragement and enthusiasm, willing us to do what they did and finish the course in fine style. The difference is, of course, that in a race the runners are competing against one another, whereas in the journeying of God's people what matters most to each runner is that all the others make it safely home as well.

What must we do to run the race with efficiency and success? The writer continues the athletic imagery to suggest three things in particular.

First, we must get rid of any heavy weights that are slowing us down. Far too many Christians try to run the race of Christian pilgrimage while carrying all kinds of heavy baggage – anxieties about trivial concerns, ambitions to use the gospel as a means of self-advancement, resentments at other people, secret greed for the bodily appetites and so on. In particular, it's possible for sin of one sort or another to get in the way and constrict our movement; though some translations speak here of sin 'clinging closely' to us, the word properly means 'obstructing' or 'constricting'.

The second point is that this race, like the ten-mile run at my school, is a long haul, and you need patience. There are always some runners who really prefer a short sprint; some of them, faced with a ten-mile run, will go far too quickly at the start and be exhausted after two or three miles. Sadly, many of us will know Christians like that too: keen and eager in their early days, they run out of steam by the time they reach mature adulthood, and by the time they're in middle age or older they have either lost all energy for active Christian living or are frantically trying to recapture the zip and sparkle of a now inappropriate teenage-style faith. Give me the person, any day, who starts a bit more slowly but who is still there, patiently running the next mile and the next and the next, all those years later.

The third point is to keep your eyes, or at least your imagination (when you're too far away to see!), fixed on the finishing line and on the one who is at the centre of the cloud of witnesses, waiting there to greet you himself. Jesus ran this course before us. In fact, he pioneered the way, opened up the course and brought it to a successful completion. Our task is to follow in his steps. He has made it across the finishing line, and his encouragement, and the thought of his welcome and congratulations at the end, are the central motivation for us to continue in hope, faith and patience.

The rest of the passage invites us to contemplate what exactly Jesus went through on his own patient journey, and to realize that we have mostly had an easy time of it by comparison. He kept his eye on the joy that was waiting for him – the joy of doing his father's will, of bringing his saving purpose to fulfilment – and he put up with the foul torture of crucifixion, a degrading and disgusting as well as excruciating and agonizing death. Hebrews is keenly aware that the readers are in danger of being weary with all that they face, day after day, in terms of threats, persecution, intimidation and mockery from their contemporaries, their neighbours and perhaps their former friends. This is like the long, hard haul up a steep and muddy hill in the middle of a long-distance race. They must keep going; they must remind themselves continually of the one who blazed this trail in the first place; they must think how much worse it was for him. That way they will be kept from becoming worn out completely. As so often in the Christian life, *reminding* yourself of *truth*, not trying to conjure up feelings of this or that sort, is the way to keep going in faith and patience.

For Reflection or Discussion

What baggage are you carrying from day to day in your Christian life? And what obstacles do others put in your way?

WEEK 2: THURSDAY

The Effect of Patience: James 1.1–8

[1]James, a slave of God and of the Lord Jesus the Messiah, to the twelve dispersed tribes: greeting.

[2]My dear family, when you find yourselves tumbling into various trials and tribulations, learn to look at it with complete joy, [3]because you know that, when your faith is put to the test, what comes out is patience. [4]What's more, you must let patience have its complete effect, so that you may be complete and whole, not falling short in anything.

[5]If any one of you falls short in wisdom, they should ask God for it, and it will be given them. God, after all, gives generously and ungrudgingly to all people. [6]But they should ask in faith, with no doubts. A person who doubts is like a wave of the sea which the wind blows and tosses about. [7]Someone like that should not suppose they will receive anything from the Lord, [8]since they are double-minded and unstable in everything they do.

I used to think the waves had come from far away. Standing by the sea and watching the grey-green monsters roll in, it was easy to imagine that this wave, and then this one, and then the one after that, had made the journey from a distant land. Here they were, like the Magi, arriving at last to deposit their gifts.

But of course it isn't like that. Waves are what happens when wind and tide take hold of the waters that are there all the time and make them dance to their tune. Just yesterday I stood in the bright sunshine and watched them sparkling and splashing around a little harbour, making the boats dip and bob. A fine sight; the waves seem to have character and energy of their own.

But they don't. They are the random products of other forces.

The challenge of faith is the challenge not to be a wave. There are many winds and tides in human life, and it's easy to imagine ourselves important because we seem, from time to time at least, to dance and sparkle this way and that. The question is whether the character that develops within us is the real thing, or whether, as James says in verse 6, we are simply double-minded and unstable, blown and tossed about by this wind or that.

We don't know for sure, by the way, who James was. It was as common a name in the first century as it is today. But there is a good chance that this letter was from the best-known James in the early church: James the brother of Jesus, the strong central leader in the Jerusalem church over the first 30 years of Christianity. Peter and Paul and the others went off around the world, but he stayed put, praying and teaching and trusting that the God who had raised his beloved brother from the dead would complete what he had begun. This letter, then, would be part of that work, written to encourage Christians across the world – whom he saw as the new version of the 'twelve dispersed tribes' of Israel – to face up to the challenge of faith.

Quite a challenge it was then, as it is now and always has been. The moment you decide to follow Jesus is the moment to expect the trials to begin. It's a bit like opening the back door to set off on a walk and finding that the wind nearly pushes you back inside before you've even started. And James tells us we should celebrate such moments (verse 2)! We should learn to look at them with joy. What can he mean?

45

When a Christian is tested it shows something real is happening. There are many kinds of test: actual persecution, which many face today; fierce and nasty temptations, which can strike suddenly when we're not expecting them; physical sickness or bereavement; family or financial troubles; and so on. But you wouldn't be tested unless you were doing something serious. Mechanics don't test scrap metal; they test cars that are going to face tough conditions. Those who follow Jesus the Messiah are not simply supposed to survive. They are supposed to count, to make a difference in the world, whether through the quiet daily witness of a faithful and gentle life or the chance, given to some, to speak and act in a way which reveals the gospel to many others. For all of that we need to become strong, to face up to the challenge.

So James draws attention to the result of the test: patience. Don't panic. Don't over-react. Don't turn a problem into a crisis. Be patient. This is one of the great themes of this letter. And, says James, you should let patience have its complete effect. Let it work right through your system (verse 4). Imagine your life like a house. Faith is what happens when you look out of the window, away from yourself, to the God who is so much greater than you. Patience is what happens inside the house when you do that.

One of the other great themes of the letter comes here at the beginning, in parallel with patience. Wisdom! James is the most obvious representative in the New Testament of what in the ancient Israelite scriptures (the Old Testament) we think of as 'wisdom literature': the sifted, tested and collected wisdom of those who learned to trust God for everything and to discover how that trust would work out in every aspect of daily life. How should I cope with this situation, with that tricky moment? You need wisdom – and you should ask for it.

But how do I know that God will give it to me? Here, as the secret of faith, patience and wisdom combined, we have the heart of what James wants to say. God gives generously and ungrudgingly to all people (verse 5). How easy it is for us to imagine that God is stingy and mean. We project on to the maker of all things the fearful, petty or even spiteful character we meet so often in real life, sometimes even when we look in the mirror. Learning who God really is and what he's truly like – and reminding ourselves of it regularly – is the key to it all. Without that, you'll be double-minded, swept this way one minute and that way the next. You'll just be another wave. With it, you will have a settled character. Wisdom. Patience. Faith.

For Reflection or Discussion

What tests have you experienced in your Christian life? How might finding the patience to wait for God have enabled you to overcome them?

WEEK 2: FRIDAY

Patience and Trust: James 5.7–11

[7] So be patient, my brothers and sisters, for the appearing of the Lord. You know how the farmer waits for the valuable crop to come up from the ground. He is patient over it, waiting for it to receive the early rain and then the late rain. [8] In the same way, you must be patient, and make your hearts strong, because the appearing of the Lord is near at hand. [9] Don't grumble against one another, my brothers and sisters,

so that you may not be judged. Look – the judge is standing at the gates! [10]Consider the prophets, my brothers and sisters, who spoke in the name of the Lord. Take them as an example of longsuffering and patience. [11]When people endure, we call them 'blessed by God'. Well, you have heard of the endurance of Job; and you saw the Lord's ultimate purpose. The Lord is deeply compassionate and kindly.

When my sister and I were reckoned to be old enough not to need a babysitter any more, my parents occasionally went out for the evening, leaving us on our own. Normally this worked fine. We could see to ourselves, the front door was locked, and in any case the world seemed a safer place in those days. But one evening, for some reason, I began to worry. I have no idea why, but instead of going to sleep as usual I stayed awake and fretted. Surely they would come soon! I guessed my parents' likely time of return; it came and went, and still no sign of them. I could hear cars on the main road, and I listened eagerly for one to turn up our street. Occasionally one did – but then it drove on by. After a while all sorts of thoughts crept over me. Supposing something had happened to them? What if there had been an accident? Perhaps they wouldn't come, not that night, not ever? I think my sister must have been asleep by then, because she would have told me not to be silly, but I ended up sitting by the window, cold with fear, hardly able to believe it when eventually the car turned up our road, stopped, and there were my parents safe and sound after a good evening, and puzzled that I would have been anxious.

I suspect that when Jesus finally appears many of us will have the same sense as I did then: how could we have been so foolish as to doubt it? How could we think that, just because it was later than we had wanted and hoped, it might mean he would never come at all? Every generation of Christians has prayed that he would come, as he promised, and so far every generation has had to learn the lesson of patience. Indeed, the command to be patient, and the fact that patience is one of the key aspects of the spirit's work in our lives, might in itself tell us that such a precious gift is going to be needed. We shouldn't be surprised at the delay. The Jewish people, after all, lived with exactly that problem through the long centuries when they wanted their Messiah to come and sort everything out, and some of them had begun to believe that the promises hadn't after all meant what they said.

Once again it's a matter of humility. Don't imagine that our timescale corresponds to God's timescale. Think of it like a farmer. Some weeks ago I watched a local farmer ploughing his field and sowing his crop. I can see the field as I write this: nothing seems to have changed (except for the fact that the gulls that followed the plough are no longer there). The soil looks just as bare as it did when he went to work. So was he wasting his time? Has the crop failed? Of course not. It just takes time, more time than we might like. Farmers learn to live with the rhythm of the seasons. Our frantic modern society, which wants to have every vegetable in the shops all year round and so brings them in by plane from far away, has done its best to obliterate the need for patience. It's all the more important that we who follow Jesus should learn it and practise it.

The way to do this is, as usual in James, to focus our attention on God himself. 'The Lord', he says, 'is deeply compassionate and kindly.' How hard it is to believe that – but how vital. How easy it is, by contrast, to think of God as remote, uncaring, unfeeling – or, if he feels anything, perhaps (we think) he's annoyed or cross with us about this or that. Well, there may be things to sort out, but God's mercy is sovereign. That is the deepest truth about him.

That was the truth glimpsed by the great prophets of old. Through long acquaintance with God himself, they had learned to see the truth behind the way things seemed, to see the heavenly dimension of ordinary earthly reality, to see the heavenly timescale intersecting with the earthly one. Job is a supreme example, but there were many others who, as the letter to the Hebrews insists, went on faithfully even though they had not themselves received the things which had been promised. A hasty, impatient spirit is another form of pride, of the human arrogance that imagines it knows better than God.

And, once more, this patience and trust must issue in appropriate speech. Again, there is a warning about grumbling against one another (verse 9): clearly this was quite a problem in James's church. Sad though this is, we shouldn't be surprised. The early Christians in Jerusalem and the surrounding area had suffered persecution ever since the death of Stephen (Acts 7). When groups and fellowships find themselves under threat from the outside, the fear and anxiety can easily breed quarrels and grumbles on the inside as well. Patience with one another is a further aspect of humility.

For Reflection or Discussion

Have you experienced grumbling or quarrelling in your church? How might the words of James here have enabled you to overcome it?

WEEK 2: SATURDAY

Patience in Prayer: James 5.13–20

[13]Are any among you suffering? Let them pray. Are any cheerful? Let them sing psalms. [14]Are any among you sick? They should call for the elders of the church, and they should pray over the sick person, anointing them with oil in the name of the Lord. [15]Faithful prayer will rescue the sick person, and the Lord will raise them up. If they have committed any sin, it will be forgiven them. [16]So confess your sins to one another, and pray for one another, that you may be healed.

When a righteous person prays, that prayer carries great power. [17]Elijah was a man with passions like ours, and he prayed and prayed that it might not rain – and it did not rain on the earth for three years and six months. [18]Then he prayed again, the sky gave rain, and the earth produced its fruit.

[19]My dear family, if someone in your company has wandered from the truth, and someone turns them back, [20]know this: the one who turns back a sinner from wandering off into error will rescue that person's life from death, and cover a multitude of sins.

There are many things in life which look extremely odd to someone who doesn't know what's going on. Imagine watching someone making a musical instrument if you'd never heard music in your life. What, you might think, can such an object possibly be for? Why waste such time and effort on it? Or imagine a child, who has no idea about babies and where they come from, or of the fact that his mother is expecting one soon, watching her get the room ready for the new arrival. It makes no sense. Why this little cot? Why these new decorations?

Of course, when the moment comes all is explained. But sometimes you have to wait; to be patient; to trust that things will come clear. James uses other examples, too, the farmer and the harvest being the obvious one. This theme of patience, which runs through the whole letter, marks his thinking out from the ordinary moralism of his day. James is constantly aware of living within a story – living, in fact, within God's story; and of the fact that this story has already reached its climax in his brother Jesus and will one day complete what he has so solidly begun.

This is the setting within which prayer, that most incomprehensible of activities, makes sense. To someone with no idea of God, of there being a world other than what we can touch and see, prayer looks at best like an odd superstition and at worst like serious self-deception. Fancy just talking to yourself and thinking it will make a difference to anything! But almost all human traditions, right across history and culture, have been aware of other dimensions which seem mysteriously to intersect with our own. The ancient Jewish tradition, which comes to fresh and vital expression in Jesus himself and in his early followers and family, sharpens up this general vague awareness of Something Else into not only Someone Else but a named Someone: the God we know in, through and as Jesus himself. Then, suddenly, prayer, and the patience which it involves, make all the sense in the world.

Prayer must surround everything else that we do, whether sad or happy, suffering or cheerful. The Psalms are there, to this day, as the natural prayer book of Jesus' followers (verse 13), even though many Christians today seem to ignore them altogether. Anointing with oil is there, to this day, as a very simple yet profound and effective sign of God's longing to heal people. Like prayer itself, such an act is mysterious; yet, for those who take what James says seriously, it is full of meaning and power. And forgiveness is there, to this day, as the great open door, the fresh possibility, the chance of a new start, for all who will confess the sin which is dragging them down, and will join in prayer for healing.

James seems, again like Jesus himself, to have seen a connection between sin and ill-health. Jesus has warned (in John 9) against making too close a link, but at other times, for instance in Mark 2.1–12, it seems that forgiveness and healing go hand in hand. Maybe these are the two things which push to the fore when we take our stand in the place where prayer makes sense, at the place where heaven and earth overlap, and at the place where our own present time and God's future time overlap.

That is, after all, what Christian prayer, and for that matter Christian sacraments, are all about. Prayer isn't just me calling out in the dark to a distant or unknown God. It means what it means and does what it does because God is, as James promised, very near to those who draw near to him. Heaven and earth meet when, in the spirit, someone calls on the name of the Lord. And it means what it means and does what it does because God's new time has broken into the continuing time of this sad old world, so that the person praying stands with one foot in the place of trouble, sickness and sin and with the other foot in the place of healing, forgiveness and hope. Prayer then brings the latter to bear on the former.

To understand all this may require some effort of the imagination. But once you've grasped it, prayer, like that puzzling musical instrument, can begin to play the tune it was designed to play. Suddenly it all makes sense.

That is why James alerts us to the great example of prayer, the archetypal prophet Elijah. There are many lessons one might draw from the story in 1 Kings 17 and 18, but we might not have grasped the point that James is making: that the drought which came as judgment on the people of Israel, and the rain which came when they returned to the Lord and abandoned their idols, all happened in the context of Elijah's prayer. And prayer, of course, is not only a task for the 'professionals', the clergy and Christian leaders. Every Christian has not only the right but the vocation to engage in prayer like that, prayer for one another, prayer for the sick, prayer for the sinners, prayer for the nation and the world. If everyone who reads these words were to determine to devote half an hour every day to this task, the effect could be incalculable.

As ever, James brings things right down to the practical level as he finishes. Once the lesson has been grasped, that in prayer the Christian stands at the overlap point of heaven and earth, of the present and the future, there is pastoral work to be done. To see someone wandering off in a dangerous direction and do nothing about it is a tragic dereliction of duty. It may be hard to turn that person back – she may insist that she is right and we are wrong! – but the effort must be made, precisely in the humility and patience which James has been urging all through. When that is done, a bit of heaven arrives on earth; a bit of God's future becomes real in the present. New life and forgiveness are there in person.

For Reflection or Discussion

Can you think of times when prayer felt like an empty activity? How might James's approach have helped you at such moments?

WEEK 3: A TIME FOR HUMILITY

THIRD SUNDAY OF ADVENT

The Example of John: John 1.6–8, 19–28

⁶There was a man called John, who was sent from God. ⁷He came as evidence, to give evidence about the light, so that everyone might believe through him. ⁸He was not himself the light, but he came to give evidence about the light . . .

¹⁹This is the evidence John gave, when the Judaeans sent priests and Levites from Jerusalem to ask him, 'Who are you?'

²⁰He was quite open about it; he didn't try to deny it. He said, quite openly, 'I am not the Messiah.'

²¹'What then?' they asked. 'Are you Elijah?'

'No, I'm not,' he replied.

'Are you the Prophet?'

'No.'

²²'Well, then, who *are* you?' they said. 'We've got to take some kind of answer back to the people who sent us. Who do you claim to be?'

²³'I'm "a voice calling in the desert",' he said, '"Straighten out the road for the master!"' – just as the prophet Isaiah said.

²⁴The people who had been sent were from the Pharisees. ²⁵They continued to question him.

'So why are you baptizing', they asked, 'if you aren't the Messiah, or Elijah, or the Prophet?'

²⁶'I'm baptizing with water,' John replied. 'But there is someone standing among you that you don't know, ²⁷someone who is to come after me. I'm not good enough to undo his sandal-strap.'

²⁸This took place in Bethany beyond the Jordan, where John was baptizing.

'I want to make it quite clear that I'm not a candidate.'

You hear that said over and over as politicians jostle for position before a major election. No, they aren't going to stand. No, they have no intention of running for office. No, they are going to sit this one out. And then – surprise, surprise – suddenly they make a speech saying that friends have advised them, that pressure has been put on them, that for the good of the country they now intend . . . to run after all. And we have become quite cynical about it all.

But here we have a story about a man pushing himself forward in the public eye, gaining a large following, and then refusing to claim any of the offices his followers were eager to ascribe to him. John, the writer of this Gospel, assumes that we know a certain amount about the 'offices' or leadership characters that many Jews were expecting at the time. The Messiah: well, of course. The king from the house of David. The king who would overthrow all injustice and rule over Israel, and perhaps the world too. But John denies quite firmly that he is the Messiah, and seems to mean it. He isn't doing messianic things.

But what about Elijah and 'the Prophet'?

For centuries the Jews had read in the Bible that the great prophet, Elijah, would return before the great and terrible 'day of the Lord' (Malachi 4.5). Elijah, it seemed, hadn't died in the ordinary way, but had been taken up to heaven directly (2 Kings 2). Now, many believed, he would return to herald God's new day. Indeed, many Christians, and most likely Jesus as well, believed that John was in fact Elijah, even if he didn't think so – a puzzle to which the New Testament offers no solution (see e.g. Mark 9.13). But, anyway, John clearly didn't want anyone thinking he was Elijah.

Elijah wasn't the only great prophet. Most in Jesus' day would have ranked him second to Moses himself. In Deuteronomy 18.15–18 God promises that he will raise up a prophet like Moses to lead the people. This figure, a yet-to-come 'prophet like Moses', was expected in Jesus' day, though most people probably didn't distinguish sharply between the different 'figures' they had heard or read about. Enough to know that *someone* would come, and preferably soon, to sort out the mess they were in.

But John refused all such titles. A group of priests and Levites – Temple functionaries – came to check him out, sent by the Pharisees who were one of the leading pressure groups of the time. They had their own reasons for wanting to keep tabs on people. If someone was behaving in a strange new way, announcing a message from God, they wanted to know about it. And John was indeed behaving strangely. Israel's scriptures hadn't spoken of a prophet who would come and plunge people into water. Why was he doing it?

John's answer, here and in what follows, is that he is getting people ready for someone else. The one claim he makes – apart from his belief that Israel's God has commanded him to baptize people in water – is that he is a 'voice'. Or rather, *the* voice, the voice spoken of by Isaiah, in the same passage where he speaks of the grass withering but the Word of God standing for ever (40.1–8). John wants us to make the connection with verses 1–18. And what the voice commands is to get the road straightened out. The master is coming; the way must be prepared.

I used to live near a busy city street, and several times a day I would hear sirens blaring as a police car, or a fire engine, or an ambulance, tried to make its way through heavy traffic to yet another emergency. That's the sort of task John claims to have: sounding his siren to clear a path for the one who's coming behind him.

John the Baptist occupies a position like this in all the gospels, and indeed within the early Christian proclamation as a whole. The movement looked back to John as its launch pad. At the same time, there were some groups of John's followers who, for whatever reason, never made the transition to following Jesus. It's possible that the writer, aware of such groups, was wanting to emphasize that John the Baptist insisted that people should follow Jesus, not himself. And he really meant it.

One of the many points to ponder about the strange character of John the Baptist is the way in which all Christian preachers are called to the same attitude that John had. We don't preach ourselves, as Paul said, but Jesus Christ as Lord, and ourselves as your servants for his sake (2 Corinthians 4.5). Or, as John put it, 'I'm only a voice.' There is his humility, and his true greatness.

For Reflection or Discussion

In what way do you preach as a servant for Jesus' sake? How far do you follow the example of John the Baptist in this?

WEEK 3: MONDAY

Boasting in the Lord: 1 Corinthians 1.26–31

[26]'Think back to your own call, my brothers and sisters. Not many of you were wise in human terms. Not many of you were powerful. Not many were nobly born. [27]But

> God chose the foolish things of the world to shame the
> wise; God chose the weak things of the world to shame
> the strong; [28]God chose the insignificant and despised things
> of the world – yes, even things that don't exist! – to abolish
> the power of the things that do exist, [29]so that no creature
> could boast in God's presence. [30]Who and what you now are
> is a gift from God in King Jesus, who has become for us God's
> wisdom – and righteousness, sanctification and redemption
> as well; [31]so that, as the Bible puts it, 'Anyone who boasts
> should boast in the Lord.'

There is a true but sad story about Cosmo Gordon Lang,
Archbishop of Canterbury from 1928 to 1942. In his day
there was no compulsory retirement age for archbishops;
but, when he reached his late seventies, realizing that he
was becoming physically frail, he decided to leave office.
At the same time, in a revealing remark to a colleague, he
showed his real fear, a fear which one might have hoped
an archbishop would long since have outgrown: 'Having
been Somebody,' he remarked, 'I shall now be Nobody.'

The world is full of 'somebodies' and 'nobodies', and it
does neither of them any good. That's not the way God
intended it to be. Every human being, man, woman, child,
and even unborn child, bears the image and likeness of
God, and none of them have either more or less dignity
because some other people have heard of them, look up
to them, or think they're special. But in most parts of
the world, at most periods of history – and, as the story
shows, often enough in the church itself – people feel that
it's better to be 'somebody'. The cult of fame has reached
monstrous proportions in recent days, to the absurd point
where many people are now famous for being famous. We
know their names, we recognize their faces, but we can't

remember whether they are footballers, film stars or fashion models. Or perhaps even archbishops.

Corinth, as a proud Roman city, was exactly the sort of place where people would look up to the 'somebodies', and do their best to join them. Then, as now, there were the obvious routes to fame: political power, and royal or noble birth. And, at Corinth (though this doesn't hold for all cultures), they paid special attention to people who could speak well: public rhetoricians, lawyers and the like. The wise, the powerful, the noble: these were the 'somebodies' in Corinth.

Paul reminds his readers that most of them were, on the same scale, 'nobodies'. When he first came to town and announced the gospel of King Jesus as Lord, and they believed it, most of them weren't among the 'wise' whom society looked up to. Most of them didn't have any social power (though Erastus, the city treasurer, is mentioned as a Corinthian Christian in Romans 16.23). Most of them didn't come from well-known, 'noble' families.

'But God . . .' Those are some of Paul's favourite words. He often describes a human situation or problem and then takes delight in showing that God has stepped in and done something to change it drastically. They were 'nobodies', but God has made them 'somebodies'. Not the sort of 'somebodies' the world would recognize as such, but the only sort that mattered. And what is important in this paragraph is the fact that God has taken the initiative in it all. The Christian gospel is a matter of grace from start to finish. God chose these Corinthian 'nobodies' (verses 27, 28); God 'called' them through Paul's announcement of the crucified Jesus as Lord (verse 26; the word 'call' is Paul's regular word for what we sometimes call 'conversion');

God gave them the status in his eyes that the Messiah himself has (verse 30). They are who they are, as he says in a rather shorthand way, 'from God in the Messiah' (verse 30). He is the one 'in whom' Christians possess all the wisdom they need – and the status ('righteousness') of being his forgiven, justified people, and the extraordinary privilege of being set apart for his service ('sanctification') in virtue of his 'redemption' of them from the slavery of sin.

The biblical theme which Paul is drawing on here is the theme of 'Wisdom'. In the book of Proverbs, in particular in its great introduction (chapters 1—9), we find Wisdom as a person, the one through whom the world was made, inviting humans to discover who she is and so to become the genuine human beings they were meant to be. Later Jewish writings like Ecclesiasticus ('The Wisdom of Ben Sirach', probably written about 200 BC) and 'The Wisdom of Solomon' (probably early first century AD) developed this idea into the notion that Wisdom is to be found in the Jewish law, or in the presence of YHWH in the Temple, and that by following this Wisdom people can be and do what God intended them to be and do in the world. For Paul, Jesus the Messiah is the true wisdom (see, e.g., Colossians 1.15–20; 2.1–3). Having him – or rather, being 'in him' – means that you are a genuine human being at last, called to live by God's wisdom rather than that of the world.

Exploring what it means to be 'in the Messiah', so that what is true of him is true of you, is the Christian's basic strength and delight. God has vindicated Jesus in his resurrection; God set him apart for his own service; God accomplished in him the defeat of the great enslaving powers of sin and death. If you are 'in Christ', a member of the Messiah's family, this 'wisdom – and righteousness, sanctification and redemption' are yours too. And if that doesn't make you 'somebody', nothing ever will.

For Reflection or Discussion

How far do you feel yourself to be either 'somebody' or 'nobody'? How far do you feel yourself to be 'in Christ'?

WEEK 3: TUESDAY

Bearing One Another's Burdens: Galatians 6.1–5

[1]My dear family, if someone is found out in some trespass, then you – the 'spiritual' ones! – should set such a person right, in a spirit of gentleness. Watch out for yourselves: you too may be tested. [2]Carry each other's burdens; that's the way to fulfil the Messiah's law. [3]If you think you're something when you are not, you deceive yourself. [4]Every one of you should test your own work, and then you will have reason to boast of yourself, not of somebody else. [5]Each of you, you see, will have to carry your own load.

I was reading the autobiography of a world-famous cricketer. He described how for his first ten years in the game the team he played for never succeeded in winning a major trophy. They had star players, many of them of much better quality than most other teams. But they were all out for themselves, their own success, their own reputation.

After those ten years, some of the senior players retired, and a younger team, less well known, emerged. A new captain was appointed, not such a famous cricketer, but determined to pull the side together. They began to work as a team. The stars were still able to perform, but the key thing was that every single player began to work for the good of the whole. If they saw another player making a mistake they would help him instead of sneering. If someone was having a difficult patch they would encourage him instead of being glad that they could shine instead. And so on. And the miracle happened: at last, the team won the championship.

The crisis in Galatia had left the church like the first of those teams. People saw themselves as one particular 'type' of Christian, and looked down on other types. If they saw one of the others doing something wrong, they would feel smug; that, they would think, is not the way 'we' behave. At the same time, these groups were defined in terms of status, not detailed behaviour; 'we' (the Jewish Christians among them? or perhaps the richer Christians? or the ones who were Roman citizens?) were simply different because they were different. Instead of the community Paul had established, where all were equal at the foot of the cross, all equally 'in Christ', all equally members of Abraham's family (Galatians 3.26–29), the work of the 'agitators' had left a legacy of division based on non-theological factors.

It is desperately easy for this kind of attitude to creep in to any church. Divisions in the wider society (caste, class, income, colour, the sort of home you live in) can quickly lead one group of Christians to look down on another. Often the others sneer back. What has that got to do with the kingdom of God?

The church is meant to work like a first-rate team. Every member should care for everyone else. Paul has just sketched out what life should be like if people are lining up with the spirit; now he applies this to the church's own inner life. He is careful not to accuse individual people, though there probably were some in the church who had been particularly at fault. He gives them, rather, general instructions which might be relevant to any church, and lets them work out for themselves where there is someone specific to whom it might apply.

This, too, is done with a smile in relation to the long earlier argument. You want to fulfil the law, do you? Very well: but let it be the law of the Messiah! This doesn't mean (as some have thought) that Jesus' teaching constituted a 'new law' to replace the law of Moses. To be sure, Jesus said many things about how his followers should behave. The church must take all such things utterly seriously. But the 'law' in question here is the law of love, the law of giving oneself in love and humility to the service of others. This, rather than showy behaviour which highlights one or two individuals, will be the sign that they are really 'spiritual'.

So, as Jesus the Messiah carried the cross for others, so Christians must carry one another's burdens. If my neighbour sins today, and I notice it, I must remember that it may well be me tomorrow. If it is my responsibility to help to put things right, I must do it without arrogance. If you think you are 'something', someone special, someone above the common run and rule of Christian living, able to look down on the others from a great height – why, then that attitude itself is evidence that you are not. You are deceiving yourself – but probably nobody else.

Here is the paradox of genuine community living. All for each and each for all; but one cannot slide through, hoping that other people's devotion and godliness will suffice, and that one does not need to worry about oneself.

When it comes to my neighbour, I must be sure to remain humble if I offer help; when it comes to myself, I must recognize my own responsibility for my actions. 'Bear one another's burdens' (verse 2) is balanced by 'each of you must carry your own load' (verse 5).

Of course, churches are not like sports teams. They are not in competition with each other, and any suggestion of such a thing is already a step down the hill towards the unspiritual life that the Galatians were courting. But, granted that, any church that takes these verses seriously will be on the way to the only victory that counts: the victory of the cross of the Messiah, lived out in community and under the eyes of the wider world.

For Reflection or Discussion

Does your church work together as a team, or are its members playing for themselves? How might it improve the situation for you to find humility?

WEEK 3: WEDNESDAY

The Mind of the Messiah: Philippians 2.5–11

[5]This is how you should think among yourselves – with the mind that you have because you belong to the Messiah, Jesus:

> [6]Who, though in God's form, did not
> regard his equality with God
> as something he ought to exploit.

> [7]Instead, he emptied himself,
> and received the form of a slave,
> being born in the likeness of humans.

And then, having human appearance,
[8]he humbled himself, and became
obedient even to death,
yes, even the death of the cross.

[9]And so God has greatly exalted him,
and to him in his favour has given
the name which is over all names:

[10]That now at the name of Jesus
every knee under heaven shall bow –
on earth, too, and under the earth;

[11]And every tongue shall confess
that Jesus, Messiah, is Lord,
to the glory of God, the father.

When people in the ancient world thought of heroic leaders, rulers and kings they often thought of Alexander the Great (356–323 BC). At the age of 20 he succeeded his father Philip to the throne of Macedonia, quickly made himself master of all Greece, and then set about the task – to him, it seemed, quite small – of conquering the rest of the world. By the time he died at the age of 33 he had succeeded to such an extent that it made sense, within the thought of the time, for him to be regarded as divine. (He had himself suggested this.)

In Paul's world the closest equivalent to Alexander was the emperor Augustus, who had put an end to the long-running Roman civil war and had brought peace to the whole known world. It wasn't long before many grateful subjects came to regard him, too, as divine. The power of military might and the immense organizational skills required to hold the empire together made this, for them, the natural conclusion. Other rulers did their best to copy Alexander's model. This was what heroic leadership looked like in that world.

Only when we grasp this do we see just how deeply subversive, how utterly counter-cultural, was Paul's gospel message concerning Jesus of Nazareth, whose resurrection had declared him to be Israel's Messiah and the world's true Lord. He was the reality, and Alexander and Augustus were the caricature. This is what true global sovereignty looked like. Hadn't Jesus himself said something similar? 'World rulers lord it over their subjects, but it mustn't be like that with you; with you, the ruler must be the slave, because the son of man came to give his life a ransom for many' (Mark 10.42–45).

Now take this stark contrast between the pagan gods and heroes and Jesus of Nazareth, and think it through against the background of the Old Testament. Who was it who arrogantly grasped at the chance to be 'like God, knowing good and evil'? Why, Adam, of course, in Genesis 3. Of course! Alexander and Augustus were just doing what the human race has always done. But what's the solution? Well, in the Old Testament, God's people Israel are the servant-people, whose suffering obedience to God's saving plan will be the unexpected way of dealing with the world's sorry state. But Israel, too, is in slavery; Israel, too, has gone the way of Adam. In Paul's own day there were would-be rulers of Israel who seemed only too eager to go the Alexander/Augustus route. So what was to be done?

There are some things that can, perhaps, only be said in poetry, and maybe this is one of them. The poem Paul places here, at the heart of his letter, answers this question and many, many more – all in order to give the deep groundwork for the challenge to self-sacrificing unity within the church. People still debate whether Paul wrote the poem himself, or was quoting an even earlier Christian writer. What is quite apparent is that here we have a very, very early statement of Christian faith in who Jesus was and what he accomplished, at which subsequent theology has gazed in awe for its remarkably full and rich statement of what was later seen as the classic doctrine of the incarnation of God in Jesus the Messiah.

Let's clear one misunderstanding out of the way in case it still confuses anybody. In verse 7 Paul says that Jesus 'emptied himself'. People have sometimes thought that this means that Jesus, having been divine up to that point, somehow stopped being divine when he became human, and then went back to being divine again. This is, in fact, completely untrue to what Paul has in mind. The point of verse 6 is that Jesus was indeed already equal with God; somehow, Paul is saying, Jesus already existed even before he became a human being (verse 7). But the decision to become human, and to go all the way along the road of obedience, obedience to the divine plan of salvation, yes, all the way to the cross – this decision was not a decision to stop being divine. It was a decision about *what it really meant to be divine.*

Jesus retained his equality with God; the significance of the cross, for Paul, is that 'God was reconciling the world to himself in the Messiah' (2 Corinthians 5.19). The point of verses 6 and 7 is that Jesus didn't regard this equality as something to take advantage of, something to exploit. Rather, the eternal son of God, the one who became human in and as Jesus of Nazareth, regarded his equality with God as committing him to the course he took: of becoming human, of becoming Israel's anointed representative, of dying under the weight of the world's evil. This is what it meant to be equal with God. As you look at the incarnate son of God dying on the cross the most powerful thought you should think is: this is the true meaning of who God is. He is the God of self-giving love.

The poem turns on the 'and so' at the start of verse 9. This means, basically, 'therefore'. What's the connection? Why should the Jesus who did what verses 6–8 say he did be honoured in this way?

The answer is that in his incarnation and on the cross Jesus has done *what only God can do.* Here is the very heart of the Christian vision of God himself: that within the Jewish vision of one God, the creator and sustainer of the universe, we are to see different self-expressions – so different, yet so intimately related, that they can be called 'father' and 'son'.

Paul is quite clear that he's not moving away from Jewish monotheism. In verse 11 he quotes Isaiah 45.23, a fiercely monotheistic Old Testament passage ('To me and me alone, says YHWH, every knee shall bow and every tongue shall swear'). Here, then, is his point: the God who will not share his glory with anyone else has shared it – with Jesus. Jesus, therefore, must somehow be identified as one who from all eternity was 'equal with God'. And his progression through incarnation to death must be seen, not as something which required him as it were to stop being God for a while, but as the perfect self-expression of the true God.

Most people in Paul's world, besotted with an idea of the gods into which people like Alexander and Augustus could be fitted without much difficulty, were shocked beyond belief at the idea that the one true God might be known at last in the person of a crucified Jew. Many people in our world find it very difficult as well, and we might like to ask the reason why. Could it be that we, too, have allowed ourselves to slide into pagan views of what deity or divinity consist of – views that would then make it difficult to fit Jesus into them? If so, isn't it about time we did what the New Testament writers urge us to do, and what this wonderful passage poetically invites us to do: to start from Jesus himself and rethink our whole picture of God around him?

If and when we do that, we shall find of course that the picture is very challenging. This is a God who is known most clearly when he abandons his rights for the sake of the world. Yes, says Paul; and that's 'the mind of Christ', the pattern of thinking that belongs to you because you belong to the Messiah (verse 5).

For Reflection or Discussion

Has your expectation of God been coloured by modern images of secular power? How might you regain an idea of Jesus as the one who expresses his divinity through suffering?

WEEK 3: THURSDAY

Humility and Faith: James 4.1–10

[1]Where do wars come from? Why do people among you fight? It all comes from within, doesn't it – from your desires for pleasure which make war in your members? [2]You want something and you haven't got it, so you murder someone.

You long to possess something, but you can't get it, so you fight and wage war. The reason you don't have it is because you don't ask for it! ³And when you do ask, you don't get it, because you ask wrongly, intending to spend it on your pleasures. ⁴Adulterers! Don't you know that to be friends with the world means being enemies with God? So anyone who wants to be friends with the world is setting themselves up as God's enemy. ⁵Or do you suppose that when the Bible says, 'He yearns jealously over the spirit he has made to dwell in us', it doesn't mean what it says?

⁶But God gives more grace; so it says, 'God opposes the proud, but gives grace to the humble.' ⁷Submit to God, then; resist the devil and he will run away from you. ⁸Draw near to God, and he will draw near to you. Make your hands clean, you sinners; and make your hearts pure, you double-minded lot. ⁹Make yourselves wretched; mourn and weep. Let your laughter turn to mourning, and your joy to sorrow. ¹⁰Humble yourselves before the Lord, and he will exalt you.

Schoolchildren of a certain age form exclusive friendships. Great human dramas are played out on a small scale when your daughter comes home in tears because her 'best friend' has declared she isn't her best friend any more, but has taken up with someone else. It seems for a moment like the end of the world. Such crises are often short-lived, not least because children grow out of that phase of life and learn to make friends more widely, and on a variety of levels.

But in other respects exclusivity is the very essence of a relationship. The obvious example is marriage. Various societies have experimented with polygamy, and even polyamory, but something deep in the human psyche seeks to bond with one person above all others. The temptation to stray is of course notorious and sometimes powerful, but it usually leads, if anywhere, not to multiple simultaneous relationships (or, if it does, the people concerned find themselves torn apart inside), but to a new exclusive bond.

In the Bible, the exclusive partnership of marriage is often used as an image of the exclusive claims of God on the human life, and so it is here. James uses the accusation 'adulterers!' (verse 4), not to accuse his readers of actual adultery, but to warn them that 'being friends with the world means being enemies with God'. It's such an important principle that he repeats it, almost word for word.

But what does he mean by 'the world' here, and how does 'friendship' with the world in that sense relate to what he's been saying about war, fighting and asking for things in the wrong way? By 'the world' he seems to mean, as often in scripture, 'the way the world behaves', the pattern of life, the underlying implicit story, the things people want, expect, long for and dream of that drive them to think and behave the way they do. If you go with the drift, if you don't reflect on what you're doing but just pick up habits of mind and body from all around you, the chances are you will become 'friends' with 'the world' in this sense. You will be 'normal'. It takes guts to stand out and be different. It also takes thought, decision and determination.

So why is 'friendship with the world' at the root of war and fighting? Because in 'the world' in this sense, the ultimate argument is a fist. Or a boot. Or a gun. Or a bomb. Violence, force, power – that's what counts. People may smile and appear friendly and civilized; society may appear open and generous; but if you go against them, if you challenge cherished assumptions, there are ways of making you feel their displeasure. Only today a friend told me that, after he had witnessed a robbery taking place and was called to give evidence, he had a brick thrown through his window. Violence, and the threat of more of it, is the way the world ultimately works, whether it's with small-town criminals or large-scale dictatorships.

So what would it mean to be a friend of God instead? It would mean, for a start, taming the desires that are agitating inside you for things you can't get, the desires that push you to fight, and even to kill or to make war. The desires, too, that lead you to pray for something (verse 3), but to pray simply for your own pleasures to be satisfied rather than for God's glory. And yet, James says, you claim to be God's people! That is spiritual adultery. Married to God, but having a long-running affair with 'the world'. God longs for exclusive friendship with all those who are made in his image.

In particular, James highlights a major lack in the world of his day: humility. Its opposite is arrogance: the arrogance that says that *my* desires come first, that *my* cause is so important it's worth fighting and killing for. The cure, of course, is to submit to God and resist the devil (verse 7) – rather than the other way around!

This may well mean a time of serious self-examination. Where are all these impulses coming from, these desires that are pulling me away from the God who truly longs to be my friend? Verses 8–10 (drawing near to God; cleansing hands and hearts; mourning and humility) sound to me like an agenda for at least six months of spiritual direction, or perhaps for an extended silent retreat. 'The world' will do its best to encourage you to play at doing these things. Five minutes of drawing near to God, and then quickly back to two hours of television. A brief cleansing of the hands and then back to the mud and the muck. A short, painful glance at the depths of the heart, and then we'll decide that that had better wait for another occasion. After all, we don't want to be gloomy, do we? Doesn't God want us to be joyful?

Well, yes, he does, but the road to joy is not the same as the road to self-satisfied 'happiness'. Being double-minded – a quick nod to God to keep him happy, and then linking arms with 'the world' once more – simply won't do. It may take time and effort to look God in the face and admit just how far we've been going wrong.

At the heart of this challenge there lies a promise so stupendous that I suspect most of us never really take it seriously: 'draw near to God and he will draw near to you.' That is astonishing! God is ready and waiting. He longs to establish a friendship with you, a friendship deeper, stronger and more satisfying than you can ever imagine. This, too, will take time, as any friendship worthy of the name will do. But what could be more worthwhile?

For Reflection or Discussion

Have you ever taken part in a retreat or other extended spiritual exercise? Did you find it helped you 'draw near to God' and away from 'the world'?

WEEK 3: FRIDAY

Living by Trust in God: James 4.11–17

[11]Do not speak evil against one another, my dear family. Anyone who speaks evil against another family member, or

passes judgment against them, speaks evil against the law and judges the law. But if you judge the law, you are not a doer of the law but a judge! [12]There is one lawgiver, one judge who can rescue or destroy. But who are you to judge your neighbour?

[13]Now look here, you people who say, 'Today, or tomorrow, we will go to such-and-such a town and spend a year there, and trade, and make some money.' [14]You have no idea what the next day will bring. What is your life? You are a mist which appears for a little while and then disappears again. [15]Instead, you ought to say, 'If the Lord wills, we shall live, and we shall do this, or that.' [16]But, as it is, you boast in your pride. All such boasting is evil. [17]So then, if anyone knows the right thing to do, but doesn't do it, it becomes sin for them.

One of the most memorable minor characters in C. S. Lewis's famous Narnia stories is the strange and increasingly sinister Uncle Andrew in *The Magician's Nephew*. Uncle Andrew is, in fact, the magician of the title, and his nephew Digory is the male hero of the story. To begin with, Uncle Andrew appears merely a bit odd. He is quirky, idiosyncratic, unpredictable, but no more than that. But gradually it becomes clear that he has planned a sinister plot – to get Digory and his sister Polly to try out what he believes to be magic rings. He is, it appears, too scared to try them for himself.

Well, they do try them out, and that sets the whole adventure in motion. But the truly sinister moment in the story, as Lewis must have intended, comes towards the end, when Uncle Andrew is explaining that while it might have been wrong for someone else to do what he has done, he lives in a world where a different set of rules apply. 'Men like me, who possess hidden wisdom,' he says, 'are freed from common rules just as we are cut off from common pleasures. Ours, my boy, is a high and lonely destiny.' Lewis, as so often, had his finger on a key moral point. The moment when someone says – to themselves, never mind to anyone else – that an action which would be wrong for 'ordinary mortals' is all right for them, because they are somehow set apart and different, that person has puffed themselves up with a gross form of pride, and is heading for disaster as a result.

James uses more or less exactly this argument in issuing a warning against speaking evil of a fellow Christian. He seems to have in mind the kind of slander or gossip which eats its way like a cancer through a Christian fellowship, and requires urgent treatment if it is not to prove fatal. His point is this: anyone who does such a thing is thereby implying, like Uncle Andrew, that the ordinary 'law' which applies to Christians – that they should love their neighbour as they love themselves – does not apply to them. They are above it! They can look down on such petty standards from a great height! They are, says James, 'judging the law', instead of trying to do what the law says. But to take such a stand is not just foolish and arrogant. It is to usurp the very role of God himself (verse 12). There is only one lawgiver, only one judge; and he can either rescue or destroy.

That last line may be a way of saying that only God is in a position to pass the kind of judgment that a Christian is making when he or she speaks evil of another Christian. But it may also be a warning. The lawgiver and judge can indeed rescue and destroy – and, if you have set yourself above his holy and royal law of freedom (see 1.25; 2.8, 12), you may find that you yourself are judged by that law.

The two halves of this passage are both, therefore, warning against the temptation to put yourself in the place of God. Verses 13–16 highlight this danger in relation to one's future plans. Here is a Christian who is running a small business. All right, he thinks to himself (and perhaps says to a friend), we shall go off to a different town and ply our trade there and make some money. He (or indeed she; there were independent businesswomen in the ancient world, as we know from Acts and elsewhere) thinks that the future can be planned like that, all laid out. Perhaps there is even a suggestion that, since we are now the people of the Messiah, our plans can be made more securely, because God is on our side!

Whatever the case, James again has stern words in store on that point. Don't you realize, he says, what your life is like? Think of the mist you see out of the window on an autumn morning. It hangs there in the valley, above the little stream. It is beautiful, evocative, mysterious; yes, just like a human being can be. Then the sun comes up a bit further, and . . . the mist simply disappears. That's what your life is like. You have no idea what today will bring, let alone tomorrow.

The lesson, once more, is humility. Learn to take each day as a gift from God, and to do such planning as is necessary in the light of that. This, indeed, has been built into Christian understanding to this day, so that many people will say 'God willing' or 'if the Lord wills', to make it clear that in their proposals for the future they are taking care not to usurp God's sovereignty.

The chapter then ends with a warning which is far more general, and indeed far more worrying, than what has gone before. Not to do what you know you should do is actually to sin! It isn't enough to avoid the obvious acts of sin. Once you learn the humility to accept God's royal law and to live by it, to accept God's sovereign ordering of all life and to live within that, then you will see more clearly the positive things to which you are being called. This may be a major life-decision, a question of your whole vocation and path of life. Or it may be the small spirit-given nudge to do a small act of kindness for a neighbour or stranger. But once you have had that nudge, that call, then to ignore it, to pretend you hadn't heard, is a further act of pride, setting yourself up in the place of God.

For Reflection or Discussion

Have you ever felt prompted by the spirit to a particular course of action? If so, how did you respond?

WEEK 3: SATURDAY

Humble Shepherds: 1 Peter 5.1–7

[1]So, then, I appeal to the elders among you, as a fellow-elder and a witness of the sufferings of the Messiah, and as one who will share in the glory that is to be revealed. [2]Do the proper work of a shepherd as you look after God's flock which has been entrusted to you, not under compulsion, but gladly, as in God's presence, not for shameful profit but eagerly. [3]You should not lord it over those for whom you are responsible, but rather be an example to the flock. [4]And when the chief shepherd appears, you will receive the crown of glory that won't wither away. [5]In the same way, too, the younger men should submit to the elders. But let all of you clothe yourselves with humility towards one another. You see, 'God resists the proud, but gives grace to the lowly.' [6]Humble

yourselves, then, under God's powerful hand, so that he may lift you up at the right time. [7]Throw all your care upon him, because he cares about you.

From time to time the television or the newspapers tell us that there is a crisis of 'leadership'. What that means, often enough, is that the media disapprove of the actual political leaders we happen to have at the moment, but even without that rather cynical observation I find myself anxious about discussion of 'leadership' in a vacuum. Sometimes, when I have been asked to give talks on the subject, I have begun by saying either that I don't really believe in 'leadership', or that I don't think it's the most important category – certainly not in the way it is often talked about today.

What I find is that anything worth calling 'leadership' happens, often without people thinking about it as such, when someone is so energetically and productively involved in whatever it is, whether making music or running a business, whether organizing a market stall or heading up a government department, that they communicate that energy and productivity, that enthusiasm and effectiveness, to those around them. Leadership, in other words, is a bit like friendship: it's something that happens best when you're not thinking about it, but instead about whatever you're actually doing together.

Come to think of it, 'happiness' falls into the same category. If you start the day thinking, 'Now: what will make me happy today?' you are less likely to be happy than if you think, 'Now, the sooner I can start painting that picture/ going for that walk/playing with the grandchildren the better!' I would rather belong to a group or a fellowship where the 'leader' had no idea about 'leadership', but was out-and-out committed to God and the gospel, than one where the person in charge had done three or four courses on 'leadership' but had found it left little time for studying scripture or for praying.

Now I know there's more to it than that. Any 'leadership' experts reading this will no doubt shake their heads at me as another hopeless case who just doesn't get it. But I have to say that today, whether in church or in society, what we need is people who care deeply about the state of the community and the wider society; people who have studied the relevant issues with professional attention; people who listen to what all sorts of other people have to say; and people who can articulate and communicate the vision to which they have come in such a way as to help others to share it as well. Now of course the 'experts' might say, 'But that's what we mean by "leadership".' If it is, well and good. But let's study and practise the thing itself, not some abstract category removed from reality.

What Peter is describing here is not 'leaders' but shepherds. And the point about 'shepherds' is that the best of them aren't thinking, 'How can I be a shepherd?', but, 'How can I best look after these sheep?' The focus of the good shepherd is not only on his or her own qualities but on the needs of, and potential dangers for, those he or she is looking after. That, of course, is the first main point Peter makes here (verse 2): don't think about your own profit, but rather about the needs of the flock. Peter appeals as himself an 'elder' – the word means 'senior', both in the sense of status within the community and in the sense of older in years, and the two of course often go together – who has responsibilities like this and hence knows what he's talking about.

In particular, Peter has learned well from Jesus himself the central thing about being God's under-shepherds: don't lord it over them, but be an example (verse 3). I was recently visiting a large college which trains army officers, and to my surprise and delight met, at almost every turn, the college's motto: 'Serve to Lead'. This isn't an empty slogan: they mean it, model it and teach it. Unless an officer is *serving* the soldiers in the unit – thinking about them as people, getting to know who they are, what they are afraid of, what makes them give of their best, and looking after them in those and all other ways – he will simply not be able to *lead* them in difficult or dangerous situations. Thus, whether we are talking about the 'younger men' (verse 5) or the 'elders', all should clothe themselves 'with humility'. We hear so much of humility within early Christian writing that it's easy to forget that, until this strange movement of Jesus and his followers, nobody outside a narrow strand within the Jewish tradition had regarded it as a virtue. Something has happened to generate an entirely different way of going about things.

No prize for guessing what it is that 'has happened'. *Jesus* 'has happened', has announced God's kingdom, has died and been raised and enthroned. He is 'the chief shepherd' (verse 4), who will reappear when heaven and earth are brought together at last. He will be the model, the standard by which all other 'shepherds' are to be judged. Jesus himself drew heavily on the biblical traditions about God's desire to 'shepherd' his people Israel. In a rural economy, it's hardly surprising that this is one of the standard images for the way in which either God himself, or the anointed king, are to look after the 'sheep', to make sure they are fed, and to protect them from predators. A glance at Psalm 23 or Ezekiel 34 will show where some of this comes from. A further glance at Luke 15.3–7 and John 10.1–16 will show you what Jesus himself made of it. And a glance at John 21.15–19 gives us a sharp and intimate glimpse of Peter himself being recommissioned as a 'shepherd' of Jesus' followers after the disaster of his earlier denials.

The normal 'worldly' way of 'leadership', of course, is to boss and nag, to threaten and punish. You may be able to get sheep to do what you want that way, but they will be neither happy nor healthy. Such an approach may look 'strong', but it is in fact weak. The call to be a humble shepherd is the call to the true strength in which one doesn't have to shout or bully, because the work of humble service has forged such a strong bond between shepherd and sheep that the shepherd only needs to walk towards the pasture and the sheep will follow.

For Reflection or Discussion

Do the leaders in your church demonstrate the qualities Peter explores in this passage? Do you demonstrate those qualities in your own leadership roles?

WEEK 4: A TIME FOR JOY

FOURTH SUNDAY OF ADVENT

A Joyful Blessing: Romans 16.25–27

[25]Now to him who is able to strengthen you according to my gospel, the proclamation of Jesus the Messiah, in accordance with the unveiling of the mystery kept hidden for long ages [26]but now revealed and made known through the prophetic writings, according to the command of the eternal God, for the obedience of faith among all the nations – [27]to the only wise God, through Jesus the Messiah, to whom be glory to the coming ages! Amen.

I watched as the children played in the swimming pool. The water was about four feet deep. Three of them stood side by side, with linked arms. Then they squatted down, with only their noses above water, and two others climbed on to their shoulders. Then a younger boy scrambled up on to *their* shoulders. And then, slowly but surely, the three at the bottom stood up, until the whole pyramid was nearly, very nearly, standing proudly upright.

At that moment two other children, seeing the fun, came to join in. Despite shouts of warning from some of those already involved, they tried to get in on the act, scrabbling and clutching and trying to join the little one up on the top. The whole pyramid began to wobble, and suddenly they all toppled over with legs and arms going in every direction and the most enormous splash I had ever seen in the pool.

That is, more or less, what has happened with the last sentence of this great letter. I think, actually, that Paul probably intended it this way. If he didn't – if, in other words, it just came out like that in his dictation and he didn't bother to correct it – I think he was happy with it, happy to make a final splash even though the construction of the sentence eventually gets top-heavy and falls over with legs and arms (extra phrases and clauses tagged in here and there) all over the place. Let's look at it and see how the pyramid was at least designed to work before the extra bits were added.

The bottom row of the pyramid is meant to say: 'To God be the glory for ever!' This divides up into three sections, closely linked. First, God is described in terms of what he can do for the Christians in Rome (for all Christians, of course, but Paul wants the church in Rome to know this in particular): he can give them strength through the gospel. Second, what has happened in the gospel is the fulfilment of the age-old story of God, Israel and the world. Third, this gospel has been spread around the world to bring about the obedience of faith. So far, so good.

Standing on the shoulders of these basic points are two more. First, the gospel has been made known through the prophetic writings: Paul may have in mind the Old Testament scriptures, or he may even be referring to some early Christian texts. Second, this has come about because of the command of God, the eternal one. Paul is clearly heaping up phrases which echo, or refer back to, entire sections of the letter that is now drawing rapidly to its close. So much of what he has been writing about has been to do with the way in which the long narrative of Israel has come to fulfilment and fruition in Jesus the Messiah, and with the way in which God himself, at work in and through Jesus, is now still at work through the announcement of the gospel.

What Paul then puts on top of the pyramid looks as though it's going to be: 'To the only wise God be glory for ever.' But then, like the extra child at the last minute, he realizes that he can hardly bring this letter of all letters to a conclusion without Jesus being in the very middle of it. So he adds one more phrase, which makes the whole sentence fall over, grammatically speaking, with a great splash: 'To the only wise God . . . *through Jesus the Messiah* . . . to whom be glory to the coming ages!'

Was the glory going to God, or to Jesus? Does it matter? Paul would certainly have said, 'No, it doesn't.' Throughout this letter Paul speaks of the living God revealing himself in, as and through Jesus. Jesus dies as the personal expression of God's love; Paul draws on the messianic language of 'son of God' as a way of expressing this close identity while still allowing for what later theologians would speak of as differentiation within the persons of the Trinity. Jesus is both Israel's Messiah according to the flesh and also 'God over all, blessed for ever'. Paul takes Old Testament passages which clearly refer to 'the Lord', meaning YHWH, the God of Israel, and transfers them so that they now refer to Jesus. What theologians call a 'high Christology' – a view of Jesus which sees him as fully and completely divine as well as fully and completely human – doesn't have to wait for later centuries and writers. It is already fully present in Paul, not least in this, his greatest letter.

In particular, we note that Paul refers in the closing phrases to God as 'the only wise God'. There were many other claims to wisdom in the ancient world. There were many other gods who offered insight, of a sort and at a cost. There were plenty of teachings about how to live, how to think, what to believe, how to pray. But Paul believes – and the powerful gospel of Jesus bears him out – that there is only one God who is truly wise. He is the creator. He understands how the whole world works, what humans are and how they think, where they go wrong and how they can be put to rights, and how, when that happens, the whole of creation will dance for joy at its new-found freedom.

This is the hidden wisdom which formed the secret plan, the plan now unveiled in the gospel, the gospel which now evokes as its proper response 'the obedience of faith' (as in 1.5), the faith which is open to the whole world. When you see the end from the beginning in this way; when you glimpse even a little of what Paul has glimpsed of the wisdom, love, grace, power and glory of the eternal God revealed in Jesus the Messiah – then you, too, will want to join him in joyfully piling up all the glory and praise and love and adoration you can muster. And you won't care how big a splash you make as you do so.

For Reflection or Discussion

Have you ever found your words running away with you through emotion? Were you able to glimpse the glory of God in this?

WEEK 4: MONDAY

The God Who Comforts the Downcast: 2 Corinthians 7.2–10

[2]Make room for us! We haven't wronged anybody, we haven't ruined anybody, we haven't taken advantage of anybody. [3]I'm not saying this to pass judgment against you; I've already said

that you are in our hearts, to die together and to live together. [4]I speak of you freely and often; I regularly boast about you; I am full of comfort, and fuller still of joy, over and above all our trouble.

[5]You see, even when we arrived in Macedonia, we couldn't relax or rest. We were troubled in every way; there were battles outside and fears inside. [6]But the God who comforts the downcast comforted us by the arrival of Titus, [7]and not only by his arrival but in the comfort he had received from you, as he told us about your longing for us, your lamenting, and your enthusiasm for me personally.

As a result, I was more inclined to celebrate; [8]because, if I did make you sad by my letter, I don't regret it; and, if I did regret it, it was because I saw that I made you sad for a while by what I had written. [9]Anyway, I'm celebrating now, not because you were saddened, but because your sadness brought you to repentance. It was a sadness from God, you see, and it did you no harm at all on our account; [10]because God's way of sadness is designed to produce a repentance which leads to salvation, and there's nothing to regret there! But the world's way of sadness produces death.

What is your image of what a successful Christian ought to look like? Do you have in the back of your mind a picture of a person who goes through life in perfect faith and trust, obedient to God in everything, never afraid of what may lie in wait around the next corner, always rejoicing even in adversity?

Do you find this image a bit depressing sometimes? It seems so unreal, so unlike not only our own lives but those of all the people we know well. Of course there are moments of joy, of celebration, of faith, of hope and of love. (At least, I hope there are.) But the course of Christian living doesn't run smoothly, and we all know it.

So where does the popular image of a 'successful Christian' come from? Well, some might say, from the New Testament. Doesn't Paul himself tell us to rejoice all the time, to praise God without ceasing, to give thanks in everything? Doesn't he say, in a famous passage in Philippians 4, that we should 'have no anxiety about anything', but should commit it all to God?

Yes, he does. But such comments need to be balanced out with deeply personal and revealing passages like the present one. If you want to know what it looks like and feels like to have no anxiety about anything, committing it all to God, come with Paul as he struggles along the road, exhausted and emotionally drained after his terrible experiences in Ephesus. He goes north to Troas, then across the narrow strip of water between Asia and Europe, the waterway we call the Dardanelles and he called the Hellespont, and on through Macedonia. Every step of the way he was praying and hoping, but it was a constant tussle against fears that welled up inside and opposition that attacked him all around. Every day when he didn't find Titus waiting for him was another disappointment; every day he went on, hoping for good news but bracing himself for the worst. 'Having no anxiety about anything', as far as Paul was concerned, wasn't a matter of attaining some kind of philosophically detached state where he simply didn't care. He cared, and cared passionately. I think 'having no anxiety' meant, for him, taking every day's anxieties and, with a huge struggle and effort, dumping them on the God in whom he doggedly believed.

The description in verse 5 of his own mental state – and the physical state which went with it, as so often the body reflects what's going on in the mind – is a great antidote to any superficial or glib statement of what a normal Christian life is like. Thank God it's not always like this; there are times when everything is going much better. But thank God that Paul, too, not just people we'd be tempted to think of as second-rate, went through periods like this, where he couldn't get any rest, and found trouble and fear inside and out. Thank God both for the time before Titus arrived, when Paul faced despair and was able to speak of it, and for the time when Titus did arrive at last, bringing good news which Paul obviously found so refreshing that we can feel his sigh of relief as he writes this paragraph.

The tables have, it seems, been turned; Paul was anxious that the Corinthians were cross with him, ready to rebel against his authority, and now Titus has made it clear that *they* are anxious about what state of mind *he* will be in when he arrives, worried that he is going to be angry with them. So he wants to assure them not only that he has been greatly comforted by news of them, but that the sorrow they felt at what had passed between them was itself an excellent thing. All of which leads him to some profound and important reflections on two different types of sadness. There is God's way of sadness and there is the world's way of sadness, and there is all the difference you can imagine between the two.

What is the difference between God's way of sadness and the world's way of sadness? The two types can be seen sharply set out in two of the central characters of the gospel story. On the night of the Last Supper, Peter followed Jesus to the high priest's house, where he proceeded to deny three times that he'd ever known Jesus. On realizing what he'd done, Peter went out and cried like a baby.

That was the first step towards the restoration that came with Jesus' appearance to him (Luke 24.34; 1 Corinthians 15.5) and the remarkable conversation with Jesus by the lakeshore (John 21.15–19). His sadness led him to repentance, and that was a cause, ultimately, for rejoicing. On the other hand, Judas, who had betrayed Jesus, showing the high priest's servants where to find him in the dark, was plunged into the darker depths of the world's way of sadness. In Matthew's account, he flings down the money he's been paid at the feet of the chief priests, and goes off and hangs himself (Matthew 27.5). Two types of sadness; two end results.

What has this passage done to our vision of normal Christian life? The answer, I hope, is that it has taken it right away from the smooth, easy picture of so much popular imagination, and has placed it alongside Paul as he goes through the strong and sudden mood swings of his journey through Macedonia; and, as well, alongside the Corinthians as they come to terms with unexpected and painful rebuke, plunging them into sadness which leads to repentance and making amends. Together Paul and Corinth make up a far more 'normal Christian life' than the standard, and almost wholly imaginary, picture. Let us not be afraid to journey with Paul, or to find ourselves in Corinth facing rebuke, knowing both God's way of sorrow and the joy of restoration.

For Reflection or Discussion

Has your experience of the Christian life ever resembled Paul's trials? How could the lessons Paul learned have helped you in your difficulties?

WEEK 4: TUESDAY

True Happiness: Philippians 2.25–30

[25]Epaphroditus . . . is my brother; he has worked alongside me and fought alongside me; and he's served as your agent in tending to my needs. [26]He was longing for you all, you see, and he was upset because you heard that he was sick. [27]And he really was sick, too; he nearly died. But God took pity on him – yes, and on me as well, so that I wouldn't have one sorrow piled on top of another.

[28]This has made me all the more eager to send him, so that you'll see him again and be glad, and my own anxieties will be laid to rest. [29]So give him a wonderfully happy welcome in the Lord, and hold people like him in special respect. [30]He came close to death through risking his life for the king's work, so that he could complete the service to me that you hadn't been able to perform.

When I was at school a first-year physics teacher once asked us the question in an examination: What are the advantages of having two eyes?

The correct answer, of course, was that with two eyes you can see things in three dimensions, and learn to judge distances, speeds and so on. One boy, however, wrote as his answer: 'Having two eyes means that you can see twice as far; and if one eye stops working you've always got the other one to fall back on!'

The teacher enjoyed this so much that he read it out to the class as a fine example of making up in ingenuity for what you lack in information. But of course the true answer remains important: with only one eye you don't get things in their proper perspective. You need two if you're to see them with all three dimensions.

The little paragraph about Epaphroditus is enormously important in helping us to get Paul and his work – and his feelings and emotions – in true perspective. If all Paul's writing was solid, dense, abstract theology we would never have known what he was really like as a human being.

Indeed, we might have had the idea that Paul lived the kind of Christian life one imagines from some popular literature: a life without stress or strain, a life of pure unmitigated joy and gladness, cheerfully doing the work of the Lord and preaching the gospel without a care in the world. Worry? Why, wasn't that sinful? Human anxieties? Why couldn't he submit them to the Lord and forget about them? Doesn't he say, in chapter 4 of this very letter, that you should rejoice at all times, commit everything to God in prayer, and know his peace which passes understanding?

Yes, he does, and that is important. But the present passage enables us to take a two-eyed look at all this; to see in three dimensions what this joy really is – and what it isn't. The passage gives us a window not only on Epaphroditus – his journeys, his mission and his nearly fatal illness – but also on Paul. He was truly glad to have Epaphroditus with him, and he was truly horrified at the thought that he might die. Verse 27 is most revealing: God took pity not only on Epaphroditus (in other words, he recovered from his illness), but also on Paul, so that he wouldn't have one sorrow piled on top of another. 'Well, Paul,' we want to say. 'What was the sorrow you already had?' Presumably he would reply: 'Being in prison, and being unable to see my brothers and sisters in the Lord.'

'Why couldn't you let go of the sorrow and simply rejoice, as you're telling us to?' we might ask. 'And how can you say that if Epaphroditus had died you would have been overwhelmed with that as a second sorrow on top of your first one? Wouldn't you have wanted to rejoice that he'd gone to be with the Lord?'

Again he might reply: 'I do rejoice, and I am rejoicing. I know that God has won the victory over the powers of evil, and that he will one day fill the world with his love and justice, raising us to new life in his final kingdom. That sustains me, and I celebrate it day by day. But at the same time I love my friends, especially those who work and struggle alongside me in the prayer and witness of the gospel. We are bound together by ties of real human affection and love.

'I'm not a Stoic,' he would say. 'I don't believe that our human emotions are silly surface noise and that we should get down beneath them to a calm, untroubled state. That's not what I mean by "joy". The joy I'm talking about goes hand in hand with hope; it doesn't mean that everything is already just as it should be, only that with Jesus now enthroned as Lord we know it will eventually get there. But if, while we're waiting for that day, we pretend we don't have human emotions – we pretend that we don't *need* human emotions! – then we are denying part of what God has given us.'

We should not imagine, then, that the call to rejoice is a call to ignore or forget the multiple human dimensions of our daily lives. After all, part of Jesus' own path of humble obedience (2.6–8) was his weeping in agony both at his friend's graveside (John 11.35) and in Gethsemane (Hebrews 5.7). Would we dare rebuke Jesus himself for failing to have a pure, untroubled joy at those moments?

Paul's description of Epaphroditus, then, reminds us of the vital truth that we are all of us, whether first-century apostles or twenty-first-century converts, expected to be fully human beings, facing all that life throws at us and being honest about the results.

For Reflection or Discussion

Have you ever been faced with the possible loss of someone close to you? How might Paul's words have helped you?

WEEK 4: WEDNESDAY

Celebrate in the Lord! Philippians 4.2–8

[2]I have a special appeal which goes jointly to Euodia and Syntyche: please, please, come to a common mind in the Lord. [3](And here's a request for you too, my loyal comrade: please help these women. They have struggled hard in the gospel alongside me, as have Clement and my other fellow-workers, whose names are in the book of life.)

[4]Celebrate joyfully in the Lord, all the time. I'll say it again: celebrate! [5]Let everybody know how gentle and gracious you are. The Lord is near.

[6]Don't worry about anything. Rather, in every area of life let God know what you want, as you pray and make requests, and give thanks as well. [7]And God's peace, which is greater than we can ever understand, will keep guard over your hearts and minds in King Jesus.

[8]For the rest, my dear family, these are the things you should think through: whatever is true, whatever is holy, whatever is upright, whatever is pure, whatever is attractive, whatever has a good reputation; anything virtuous, anything praiseworthy.

You never know when it's going to happen. Two people who one day are good friends, working alongside each other in the church or community, can suddenly get across each other. A sharp word from one, half-heard by the other; a bitter response, spoken hastily and without quite meaning it; then the slamming of doors, the face turned away in the street, the sense (on both sides) of hurt so great, and offence so deep, that nothing can mend it. I remember my grandfather, a pastor himself, telling me of such things. I in my turn have had to deal with a few such incidents, and I guess most pastors have done the same.

It is particularly sad and tragic when it occurs within a Christian community where the whole ethos ought to be one of mutual love, forgiveness and support; but the chances are that since each one will accuse the other of being the first to break this code, neither is prepared to back down. It then calls for a certain amount of what in international relations is called 'shuttle diplomacy' on the part of a pastor or wise friend before any progress is made.

But a word addressed in public to both parties might just break the deadlock (though you'd have to know what you were doing; it might make it worse). We assume from verse 2 that Paul knew what he was doing. Two women in Philippi, Euodia and Syntyche, have fallen out, and he's appealing publicly for them to come to agreement.

These things are better dealt with sooner rather than later. I was talking yesterday to a sensible lady, a mother and grandmother, who told me that her golden rule was never to let more than two days' ironing pile up. After that it would be too daunting to contemplate. In the same way, something that needs to be ironed out within the Christian community should be tackled as quickly as possible, before resentment solidifies and cannot be softened and melted. The present disagreement between Euodia and Syntyche must have been going on for some time, since Paul must have heard about it from Epaphroditus. Maybe, he thinks, only a word from the apostle himself will now produce some change.

Who, then, is the 'loyal comrade' to whom he appeals for help on the ground in this pastoral dilemma? We don't know. Perhaps it was Epaphroditus himself, who was going to take Paul's letter back to Philippi; this mention here would then give him the authority to act in Paul's name. Or perhaps it was one particular church leader whom Paul knew very well and whom the rest of the church would recognize when addressed like this.

After this brief aside for a particular problem, Paul turns to his real final command before he moves towards the end of the letter. Everything comes under the great heading in verse 4: celebrate in the Lord!

Often the word here is translated 'rejoice'. We normally understand that word today, I think, as meaning something that happens inside people, a sense of joy welling up and making them happy from within. All that is important, and is contained within Paul's command; but in his world and culture such rejoicing would have meant (what we would call) public celebration. The world all around, in Ephesus, Philippi, Corinth and elsewhere used to organize great festivals, games and shows to celebrate their gods and their cities, not least the new 'god', Caesar himself. Why shouldn't the followers of King Jesus celebrate exuberantly? It's only right; and celebrating Jesus as Lord encourages and strengthens loyalty and obedience to him.

At the same time, it's interesting that Paul at once says that the public image of the Christian church should be of a gentle, gracious community (verse 5). Exuberance must not turn into mere extrovert enthusiasm which squashes sensitive souls and offends those who are by nature quiet and reserved.

The three main things that will come into line if the celebration is both joyful and gentle are the prayer which overcomes anxiety (verses 6–7); the patterns of thought which celebrate God's goodness throughout creation (verse 8); and the style of life which embodies the gospel (verse 9).

Anxiety was a way of life for many in the ancient pagan world. With so many gods and goddesses, all of them potentially out to get you for some offence you mightn't even know about, you never knew whether something bad was waiting for you just round the corner. With the God who had now revealed himself in Jesus, there was no guarantee (as we've seen) against suffering, but there was the certainty that this God was ultimately in control and that he would always hear and answer prayers on any topic whatever.

The command in verse 8, to think about all the wonderful and lovely things listed here, runs directly opposite to the habits of mind instilled by the modern media. Read the newspapers: their stock-in-trade is anything that is untrue, unholy, unjust, impure, ugly, of ill repute, vicious and blameworthy. Is that a true representation of God's good and beautiful world? You are never going to celebrate the goodness of the creator if you feed your mind only on the places in the world which humans have made ugly. Instead, fill your mind with all the things that God has given us to be legitimately pleased with – and enjoy!

For Reflection or Discussion

Have there been disagreements in your church that might have been resolved by bearing in mind Paul's advice? What things might you want to celebrate?

WEEK 4: THURSDAY

Paul's Joy and Crown: 1 Thessalonians 2.17–20

[17]As for us, my dear family, we were snatched away from you for a short time, in person though not in heart. We longed eagerly, with a great desire, to see you face to face. [18]That's why we wanted to come to you – I, Paul, again and again – but the satan got in our way.

[19]Don't you see? When our Lord Jesus is present once more, what is my hope, my joy, the crown of my boasting before him? It's you! [20]Yes: you are our glory and our joy.

There were tear-jerking scenes on the television last night. Twin baby girls had been adopted by a couple from another country, who had found the children being advertised for adoption over the Internet. But another couple, from the children's own country, thought the twins had been promised to them. Meanwhile the children's natural mother changed her mind and said she wanted them back. Then, apparently to protect the babies from any more exposure to the bright lights of the media, officials from the government's social agency took the children away for their own protection, and gave them into the care of foster parents. It was a legal, moral and emotional nightmare for all concerned.

For a little baby, to be taken away from a parent is often traumatic – though, in the televised case, the babies seemed to be the least upset of all the people involved. For a parent, to have a child taken away is agony. Even in the animal kingdom, the mother will often make a great fuss about losing a baby; how much more in the human world.

That is the image Paul uses for how he felt about having to leave the Thessalonians, once his presence in their city looked like precipitating another riot. These verses, and the whole of the next chapter, grow out of his sense of deep bonding with them, like a mother with the baby she has begun to feed. He has been snatched away from them, and his whole heart and being yearns to be face to face with them again. Any idea that Paul was a cerebral theologian only, organizing his ideas into neat patterns without being caught up in the power and glory, and the emotional ties, of the gospel, is completely ruled out by this passage.

Like an anxious parent, Paul's every thought has been how to get back to see his beloved (and, he fears, endangered) children again. As he journeys south, to Beroea, Athens and then Corinth, at every turn he is trying to work out ways of going back north to them once more. But, he says, 'the satan got in our way.' He says something similar in Romans 1.13, about his unfulfilled desire to go to Rome. What does he mean?

Paul doesn't often mention 'the satan', but when he does he seems to be aware that behind at least some of the ordinary frustrations and thwarted plans that are common to the human race we may discern a darker and more malevolent force at work. This force – it may be going too far to see it as 'personal' – embodies itself from time to time in human beings and organizations that block God's purpose or hold it up for a while. In the present case, Paul presumably means that the death threats he was receiving as he journeyed south made it quite impossible for him to return to northern Greece again just at the moment. In particular, they thwarted his deeply pastoral purpose, to care for the new little church, to teach them the way of holiness, and to bring them the comfort that a fuller understanding of the gospel would afford.

But of course if Paul had always been with his churches we would never have had his letters. His letters are a substitute for his personal presence, binding him and the churches together in a fellowship which, though not face to face as they would have liked, is nevertheless a fellowship of heart and mind. Underneath the opposition of 'the satan' we may sometimes discern the strange providence of God. This does not rob the 'satanic' opposition of danger or threat, but it reminds us that God remains sovereign even over present dark frustrations.

Paul's reason for longing to see the Thessalonians is not simply that they have become very dear to him. It also has a forward look. From this point on the letter increasingly looks ahead to the great coming day, the day when Jesus will be revealed once more and so will be personally present with his people, and as Lord of the world. And when Paul looks forward to that day, as he does eagerly, the thing that he regards as his reason for confidence, his 'boasting', in the presence of the Lord is the Christians who have become established and mature through his work. They are his 'hope, joy and crown', his 'glory and joy'.

This is remarkable for several reasons, and should be an encouragement and stimulus both to pastors and to congregations. But it might, at first glance, seem to be odd. Surely for Paul the single hope for the future, the thing that will stand him in good stead on the last day, is simply the cross and resurrection of Jesus Christ? 'God forbid', he writes in Galatians 6.14, 'that I should boast, except in the cross of our Lord Jesus the Messiah.' Has he changed his mind?

Of course not. Jesus' death and resurrection remain foundational for who Paul is and what he does (see e.g. 1 Thessalonians 4.14). But the 'boasting' he there refers to relates to his *present status*, his standing before God in faith; this is what rules out, as Galatians makes clear, all present standing based on the marks of belonging to a particular race or tribe, or on any human achievement or effort. What Paul is now talking about is his hope for the future, for the last day when, as he says in Galatians 5.6, what will count is 'faith at work through love'. For Paul, the work of love has meant the founding and nurturing of churches, as the substantial sign that the living God has indeed been at work through him.

Of course, there are thousands of different Christian callings, most of them not nearly so spectacular and obvious as Paul's. Each of us has our own work of love to perform, whether it be quiet and secret or well known and public. Each pastor and teacher should look to the future, and see those in his or her charge as a potential joy, hope and crown. And each congregation should recognize that this is how they will appear on the last day. Both should be challenged and encouraged, by this forward look, to learn and live the faith, to celebrate the hope, to consolidate and practise the love and joy revealed in the gospel.

For Reflection or Discussion

Have you ever been separated by force of circumstance from those you love? How might Paul's words help ease this separation?

WEEK 4: FRIDAY

The Great Rescue: Revelation 7.9–17

⁹After this I looked, and lo and behold a huge gathering which nobody could possibly count, from every nation and tribe and people and language. They were standing in front of the throne, and in front of the lamb. They were dressed in white robes, holding palm branches in their hands. ¹⁰They were shouting out at the tops of their voices, 'Salvation belongs to our God, to the one who sits on the throne, and to the lamb!' ¹¹All the angels who were standing around the throne and the elders and the four creatures fell down on their faces before the throne and worshipped God. ¹²'Yes, Amen!' they were saying. 'Blessing and glory and wisdom and thanks and honour and power and strength be to our God for ever and ever! Amen!'

¹³One of the elders spoke to me. 'Who are these people dressed all in white?' he asked. 'Where have they come from?'

¹⁴'Sir,' I replied, 'you know!'

'These are the ones', he said, 'who have come out of the great suffering. They have washed their clothes and made them white in the blood of the lamb. ¹⁵That is why they are there in front of God's throne, serving him day and night in his temple. The one who sits on the throne will shelter them with his presence. ¹⁶They will never be hungry again, or thirsty again. The sun will not scorch them, nor will any fierce heat. ¹⁷The lamb, who is in the midst of the throne, will be their shepherd. He will lead them to springs of running water, and God will wipe away every tear from their eyes.'

I stopped sleepwalking some time in my mid-twenties, but I can still remember the mixture of fear and excitement I used to feel when, eventually, I would wake up. In my dream, I had been in a room, in a house, in a corridor, somewhere which was part memory, part imagination. There were people there I had to meet; there were things I had to do. But then, as I gradually emerged from sleep, I had to adjust my mind and imagination to realize that, instead of the place where I had been in my dream, I was in fact in *this* room, in *this* passage, and had to navigate my way back to my bed. Often the dream would still be powerfully present, and sometimes more appealing than the humdrum reality I actually faced. But I had to tell myself that this was the reality.

Sometimes, of course, it's the other way round. Sometimes you're in the middle of a nightmare which seems so real, so powerful and so horrible that when you wake up you can hardly dare to believe that it was only a dream, that the accident didn't happen, that so-and-so is still alive after all, that the monster attacking you was just in your imagination. Again, the clash of dream and reality is powerful. To begin with, it may be difficult to tell which is which.

John was facing a similar problem with the little communities to whom he was sending this book. They were about to face a nightmare. Persecution was on the way, and they must be ready for it. What he is offering them here is part of his continuing vision; and it's a vision not of nice dreams in his head, but of the heavenly reality which is the absolute, utter truth against which the nightmare must be measured. This, he says, is the ultimate reality of the situation, and you must hold on to it for dear life as you plunge back into the nightmare. The reality is that the creator God and the lamb have already won the victory, the victory which means that those who follow the lamb are rescued from harm. The people who claim the lamb's protection may well have to come through a time of great suffering, but they will then find themselves in the true reality, in God's throne room, worshipping and serving him day and night with great, abundant and exuberant joy.

This vision, then, is the thing which John 'sees' (verse 9), after having 'heard' the list of the 144,000 in verses 4–8. Formally speaking, this is the complete people of God, 12 times 12 times a thousand. In reality, it is a huge throng which nobody could ever count (think of the journalists' estimates of a great crowd filling a city square; then multiply that crowd by a few hundred, or a few thousand, so that the counters simply give up with a smile). Clothed in white, for victory and purity, this crowd is carrying palm branches as a further sign of victory celebration, and they can't restrain their enthusiasm: they are shouting out their delight and praise and thanks to God and the lamb, because they have won the victory which has brought them their rescue.

The word 'salvation' in verse 10 literally means 'rescue'. But often in the Old Testament the word seems to mean 'the victory through which rescue is won'. So it seems to be here. The shout of praise continues into verse 12, where the great crowd of the redeemed recognize with joy that everything good, noble, powerful and wise comes from God himself. In technical language, this is what true monotheism looks like: not a bare, dry acknowledgement that there is only one God, but the uninhibited shout of praise to the God from whom all blessings flow.

There then follows one of those little conversations with which the dream-writing and vision-literature of the time is peppered. John, we remind ourselves, is in the heavenly throne room, which is also the heavenly temple, the counterpart to the Temple in Jerusalem. He is not simply looking on from a great distance in a fly-on-the-wall fashion; he is right there, with the four living creatures and the twenty-four elders. And one of those elders now speaks to him, asking him the question which John's reader wants to ask. Who are these people?

The elder himself supplies the answer – the answer that John's communities badly need to hear. *These are those who have come out of the great suffering.* They have lived through the nightmare and can now wake up to a glorious, fresh new morning. The reason their clothes are white is not because they necessarily lived lives of total holiness and purity, but because the blood of the lamb, the sacrificial Passover-like death of Jesus himself, has rescued them from slavery to sin, making them able at once to stand in the very presence of the living God. No need to wait, then; no fear of a lengthy post-mortem clean-up period. The death of Jesus, and the suffering they have already endured, have done all that is required.

God will not only allow them, welcome them, into his presence. He will '*shelter* them with his presence'. God's 'presence' is a way of speaking of his glorious presence in his Temple, and the word for 'shelter them' means literally that God will 'pitch his tent over them', as he pitched his tent in the midst of the Israelites during their wilderness wanderings. All the blessings of the Jerusalem Temple, in other words, will be theirs.

And more besides: because at this point John glimpses the further future, the vision of the New Jerusalem itself, when God himself 'will wipe away every tear from their eyes'. There is an intimacy about that promise. Yes, God is rightly angry with all those who deface his beautiful creation and make the lives of their fellow humans miserable and wretched. But the reason he is angry is because, at his very heart, he is so full of mercy that his most characteristic action is to come down from the throne and, in person, wipe away every tear from every eye. Learning to think of this God when we hear the word 'God', rather than instantly thinking of a faceless heavenly bureaucrat or a violent celestial bully, is one of the most important ways in which we are to wake up from the nightmare and embrace the reality, and the tremendous joy, of God's true day.

For Reflection or Discussion

Have you ever been faced with the certainty of great suffering to come? How might John's assurance have helped you?

WEEK 4: SATURDAY

New Heaven, New Earth: Revelation 21.1–5

¹Then I saw a new heaven and a new earth. The first heaven and the first earth had passed away, and there was no longer any sea. ²And I saw the holy city, the new Jerusalem, coming

down out of heaven, from God, prepared like a bride dressed up for her husband. ³I heard a loud voice from the throne, and this is what it said: 'Look! God has come to dwell with humans! He will dwell with them, and they will be his people, and God himself will be with them and will be their God. ⁴He will wipe away every tear from their eyes. There will be no more death, or mourning or weeping or pain any more, since the first things have passed away.'

⁵The one who sat on the throne said, 'Look, I am making all things new.' And he said, 'Write, because these words are faithful and true.'

When has there been a moment in your life when you have said to yourself, 'This is new'? I don't just mean a car with a few new gadgets, or a meal with a different combination of sauces and seasonings – though these, too, may point in the right direction. I'm thinking more of major life experiences in which we think to ourselves, 'Everything is going to be different now. This is quite new. This is a whole new world opening up.'

Such experiences might well include some major life events: birth, marriage, full recovery from a long and dangerous illness, the experience of someone new coming to live with you. All these, interestingly, feature in the list of images John uses as he builds up this breathtaking picture of the new heaven and new earth. 'I will be his God and he shall be my son' (verse 7): a final new birth. The holy city is like 'a bride dressed up for her husband': a wedding. There will be 'no more death, or mourning or weeping or pain any more': the great recovery. And, central to this whole joyful picture, and indeed explaining what it all means, is the great promise: 'God has come to dwell with humans.' The new, permanent guest.

Putting it like this is in danger of belittling John's picture, trimming it down to our comparatively trivial examples. But, as with all symbolism, these are signposts pointing into the unknown future; and at every point John is saying, 'It's like this, but much, much more so.' The new heaven and new earth will be new in a new way; newness itself will be renewed, so that instead of a mere transition within ongoing human life, what God has planned will be the renewal of all things. 'Look,' he said, 'I am making all things new.'

All things: here we have the new heaven, the new earth, the new Jerusalem, the new Temple and, not least, the new people, people who have woken up to find themselves beyond the reach of death, tears and pain. 'The first things have passed away.'

The word 'dwell' in verse 3 is crucial, because the word John uses conjures up the idea of God 'dwelling' in the Temple in Jerusalem, revealing his glory in the midst of his people. This is what John's gospel says about Jesus: the Word became flesh and lived, 'dwelt', pitched his tent, 'tabernacled', in our midst, and we gazed upon his glory. What God did in Jesus, coming to an unknowing world and an unwelcoming people, he is doing on a cosmic scale. He is coming to live, for ever, in our midst, a healing, comforting, celebrating presence. And the idea of 'incarnation', so long a key topic in our thinking about Jesus, is revealed as the key topic in our thinking about God's future for the world. Heaven and earth were joined together in Jesus; heaven and earth will one day be joined fully and for ever. Paul says exactly the same thing in Ephesians 1.10.

That is why the closing scene in the Bible is not a vision of human beings going up to heaven, as in so much popular imagination, nor even of Jesus himself coming down to earth, but of the new Jerusalem itself coming down from heaven to earth. At first sight, this is a bit of a shock: surely the new Jerusalem, the bride of the lamb, consists of the people of God, and surely they are on earth already! How can they have been in heaven as well?

The clue here is that, as Paul says in Colossians 3.3, 'our life is hidden with the Messiah in God'. When somebody belongs to the Messiah, they continue with their life on earth, but they have a secret life as well, a fresh gift from God, which becomes part of the hidden reality that will be 'revealed' at the last day (Colossians 3.4; 1 John 3.2). That is why, in those great scenes in Revelation 5, 7 and 19, there is a great, uncountable number of people standing around God's throne in heaven, singing joyful songs and shouting out their praises. This is the heavenly reality which corresponds to the (apparently) weak, feeble praises of the church on earth. *And one day this heavenly reality will be revealed*, revealed as the true partner of the lamb, now transformed, Cinderella-like, from slave-girl to bride.

The newness of this vision is not a matter of God throwing away his first creation and, as it were, trying again, having a second shot to see if he can get it right this time. What we have is the *utter transformation* of heaven and earth by means of God abolishing, from within both heaven and earth, everything that has to do both with the as-yet incomplete plan for creation and, more particularly, with the horrible, disgusting and tragic effects of human sin.

The new world, in other words, will be like the present one in the sense of its being a world full of beauty, power, delight, tenderness and glory. In this new world, for instance, the Temple, which was properly there in heaven as well as on earth (11.19), will be abolished (21.22); not because it was a stupid idea for God to dwell among his people, but because the Temple was the advance model of God's great hidden plan for the whole cosmos, now at last to be realized. The new world will be like the present one, but without all those features, particularly death, tears and everything that causes them, which make the present world what it is.

At the centre of the picture is the one true God who made the first creation and loved it so much that he sent the lamb to redeem and renew it. Up to now, 'the one who sits on the throne' has been mentioned only obliquely. He has been there; he has been worshipped; but all the talking has been done by Jesus, or by an angel, or by 'a voice from heaven'. Now, at last, God himself addresses John, and through him addresses his churches and ours.

As we contemplate this revelation of God's eternal character, as we think about how and why God came to dwell with us in Jesus, and as we look forward to the wonderful future that will one day open up before us, let us end our Advent journey by joining in the joyful praise that John heard from the heavenly Temple (7.12):

'Blessing and glory and wisdom and thanks and honour and power and strength be to our God for ever and ever! Amen!'

For Reflection or Discussion

At any moments when you thought 'this is new', can you recall how everything seemed transformed? In what ways can you see the hand of God in this?